HMS MEDWAY QUEEN

Memories of Dunkirk

Richard Halton

Published in supp
Medway Queen Pres∈

ISBN 978-1-9163570-1-3

First published 2020
Reprinted in partnership with Mainline & Maritime Ltd 2024

The New Medway Steam Packet Company (Medway Queen Preservation Society)
is a UK registered charity (No. 296236) and registered company (No. 2100358)
Medway Queen Preservation Society
Gillingham Pier
Pier Approach Road
Gillingham
Kent ME7 1RX

.

www.medwayqueen.co.uk

Printed in the UK

Cover Illustration:
*From a painting of HMS **Medway Queen** at Dunkirk by Roy Gargett. The painting
was presented to MQPS in 1990 to mark the 50th anniversary of the Dunkirk
Evacuation.*

Title page illustration:
Roy Gargett's initial sketch for the cover painting.

Contents

Foreword, Alan Cook   5

Introduction to Operation Dynamo   7

Captain's Log - Lt. Alfred Thomas Cook RNR   9

Her Finest Hour - Lt. John David Graves RNVR   15

Go to the Galley Door, boys - Thomas Russell   27

The Dunkirk crew's memories   33

Dunkirk Survivors' memories of Medway Queen   50

Jack Skinner's diary "very nearly heroes"   69

Well Done Medway Queen   73

Medway Queen today   75

Acknowledgements

As so often before, I have to thank Kevin Robertson for his invaluable help and expertise in preparing this book. Also my wife, Jane, who puts up with me huddled over the computer for hours on end - maybe she likes the resulting peace and quiet! I have attempted to acknowledge sources as I go, in the text. The stories have come from the men who were there, relayed by their descendants or recorded in the Medway Queen Preservation Society archives and publications. It is first-hand accounts such as these that bring a story to life. My grateful thanks to everyone who took the trouble to record and save this information. Thanks, also, to previous editors of the society's magazine, "Full Ahead", and its predecessor, "Medway Queen News", as well as others who prepared material for publication.

Russell Plummer's "Paddle Steamers at War" and websites such as Wikipedia and naval-history.net were very useful for checking background information. More facts have been taken from previous society publications and from the history section of www.medwayqueen.co.uk

Richard Halton

The beach at Dunkirk, Harold Slade - courtesy of Andrew and Tim Claringbull.

FOREWORD
Alan M Cook MSc RIBA

When the *Medway Queen* returned after her last trip to Dunkirk on 4th June 1940 it is said that all the ships blew their horns and Vice Admiral Ramsay in charge of Operation Dynamo signalled "well done Medway Queen... Heroine of Dunkirk". Undoubtedly she was, but only because of the courage, tenacity, sheer willpower and determination of her crew from her Captain to her deckhands. All were heroes. Her Captain was Alfred Thomas Cook DSC, my Grandfather, and I am privileged to write this foreword.

None of us standing now on the deck of the MQ can imagine what it was like to be under constant shellfire, aircraft attack, risk of hitting mines or submerged wrecks, for seven relentless trips to the beaches and quayside of Dunkirk. Not one, not two but seven trips in a slow moving day tripper pre-war paddle steamer packed to the limit with hundreds of exhausted soldiers. Her crew's selfless bravery cannot be overestimated.

Grandpa didn't talk about his experiences. He passed when I was only 12; a tough, stern but kind man whom I saw infrequently, as I lived far from his W Sussex home. His son, my Dad, Lionel Aubrey Cook MBE, was awarded the MBE and Lloyd's Medal in the Merchant Navy in 1942. He was a lieutenant in the Royal Navy chasing U-boats on a Belfast based frigate when he met my Mum at an officers' dance. My Uncle Alan was in the RAF. He was shot down over Germany and killed trying to escape from Stalag VIIIB in 1943. Auntie Pam served in the Wrens. Our family had an 'eventful' war!

I knew the story of the *Medway Queen* from an early age and had a plastic model of her in the 1960s. In 2014 I took my Grandpa's story to the BBC *Antiques Roadshow* and it became the main feature of the Hillsborough Co Down programme. Amazingly an *Antiques Roadshow Detectives* documentary followed in 2015. This started a journey of discovery from the Royal Naval Archives in Portsmouth to the *Medway Queen* herself and to meet Jim Chivers, the last known surviving soldier rescued by her.* A really emotional time matched only by the moment I first stepped onto her deck alone with my thoughts and met Sue, the daughter of Sub Lieutenant John Graves, second in command at Dunkirk. Amidst the heroics of the crew and the thousands of soldiers saved, one other was rescued! A little mongrel puppy brought on board was adopted by my Grandpa. Christened 'Dunky' she lived a happy life on the South Coast of England.

I commend everyone to read this book and support the great work of the MQPS. There is no other ship still afloat which started life as a civilian pleasure boat, became a minesweeper and ultimately played such a key part in Dunkirk at the time of the nation's greatest peril.

* Jim sadly passed away at the age of 100, in June 2018.

Photo - "Grandpa Dom" and "Dunky" - courtesy of Alan Cook

A letter received from Mr George Harrison, regarding his observation of the Dunkirk evacuation.

May 13th 2016.

Dear Richard Halton.

Thankyou for your letter of may 6th and details about The Medway Queen.

At 0745 June 1st 1940 The M.Q was about 40 yards away from the ship in which I was a 16 year old cadet. M.V. Wairangi, Shaw Savill & Albion, 12000 tons homeward bound from Australia, meat, wool & butter.

A calm Sea, many small boats and we were very slowly making our way through the evacuation., Home port London, I had my 17th birthday of June 19th.

M.V. Wairangi was sunk on the way to Malta in the Pedistal Convoy.

Best wishes to all your crew

Yours sincerely

George Harrison

Historical Note: Operation Pedestal was a re-supply convoy to the island of Malta in the Mediterranean Sea in August 1942. They suffered heavy losses, including the MV *Wairangi* on 13th August, but enough stores and fuel were delivered to keep the island going.

INTRODUCTION TO OPERATION DYNAMO

To commemorate the 75th anniversary of Dunkirk in 2015 the Medway Queen Preservation Society had the ship towed to Ramsgate to join the "Little Ships" there. This raised the project's profile and made the ship available to thousands of visitors during the commemorations. The society had hoped to repeat this expedition for the 80th anniversary but circumstances dictated otherwise. This book is a small way of commemorating the evacuation, bringing the stories of HMS *Medway Queen*'s crew and her rescued soldiers together for the first time. I do not claim to have "written" this book. It was more of an editorial function as the accounts came from those that were there.

First we should set the scene for one of World War II's most memorable battles. The "phoney war" on land ended with the Norwegian campaign and on 10th May 1940 the German Army launched its attack on France, through Holland and Belgium. On the 13th a second attack entered France at Sedan. After breaking through, German armour headed for the Channel to trap the allied armies. The allies fell back towards the coast and, with the loss of Boulogne on 25th May and Calais on the 26th, were forced into an ever smaller perimeter.

The only way out for the British was evacuation by sea. The BEF and the French First Army retreated towards Dunkirk (Dunquerque). Dunkirk had much to recommend it with a large modern port and miles of gently sloping beaches. In the event, however, most of the port was unusable and the majority of the men had to be loaded via the East Mole or from the beaches themselves.

The Royal Navy had been planning for this eventuality. Vice Admiral Bertram Ramsay was put in charge and had less than a week of preparation before the official order to begin operation Dynamo was issued at 1857 on Sunday 26th May. Before that, however, a number of troops had been evacuated by destroyers and other ships and the despatch of personnel vessels (mainly cross channel ferries) had started at 1500 on the 26th with the intention of providing two ships every four hours. The first of these returned at 2230 and landed 1,312 men. Preparations for the full scale evacuation intensified. Orders were given and stores issued. Hundreds of ships and boats were allocated to the task.

We are fortunate in that the various accounts of HMS *Medway Queen*'s part in the operation are broadly compatible with one another although dates, timings and the order of events are not always certain. Reports and statistics relating to Operation Dynamo often conflict and Admiral Ramsay in his official report states clearly that the official total of men landed is an under estimate. *Medway Queen*'s crew's own estimate of men saved, first published in Thomas Russell's account in 1974, was 7,000. The logs suggest a rather different figure but even they were written up after the event. The figure of seven trips is not disputed. Under these circumstances the crew's estimate of 7,000 rescued and three aircraft destroyed is as good a summary as any.

CAPTAIN'S LOG
Lt. Alfred Thomas Cook RNR

Lieutenant. Alfred Thomas Cook was HMS *Medway Queen*'s Commanding Officer during the Dunkirk Evacuation. His hand written "narrative" of the operation, written immediately after the event, reads as follows:

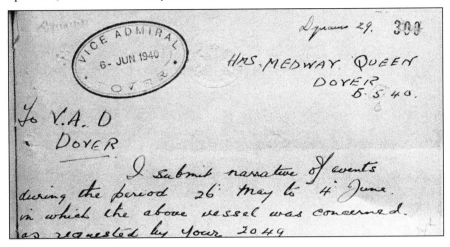

To Vice Admiral, Dover   HMS
Medway Queen
                                                          Dover
                                                          6 .6 40

I submit narrative of events during the period 26th May to 4th June in which the above vessel was concerned as suggested by your 2049.

27th May Recalled from Downs and proceeded in company with "Sandown", "Gracie Fields" and "Brighton Belle" to La Panne arriving at 2300 hrs. Evacuated 600 British troops from beach and proceeded to Ramsgate. Ship attacked off North Goodwin light by enemy aircraft. Opened fire and brought down one plane. Received SOS from H.M.S. "Brighton Belle" sinking owing to striking submerged wreck. Proceeded alongside her

*Photo: HMS **Medway Queen** in Ramsgate 1940 - courtesy of PSPS Collection.*

9

and took off troops and all members of crew. "Brighton Belle" sunk.

28th At 2045 hrs hove up and proceeded independently to Dunkirk. Arrived at 2 hrs and evacuated 450 troops. Returned to Ramsgate.

29th 1800 hrs hove up and proceeded to beach at Bray. Evacuated 450 troops and returned to Margate.

30th At 1900 left Margate and proceeded to Bray. Evacuated 550 troops. Landed them at Ramsgate.

31st Sailing orders cancelled. Ship under 1 hrs notice to proceed.

1st June at 1100 hrs proceeded beach east of Dunkirk Defence. At 1300 picked up open boat with 10 Spanish refugees. Proceeded. Evacuated 700 troops, crews of Aura and [illegible name]. Ship attacked by enemy aircraft west of Dunkirk. Opened fire and brought plane down on beach west of Dunkirk. Landed troops at Ramsgate.

2nd At 1800 hrs left Dover. At 0030 hrs took off 625 French troops from East pier Dunkirk. Landed them at Ramsgate. Commander Greig of Sandown aboard.

3rd 2000 hrs proceeded to Dunkirk took off 400 French troops landed them at Ramsgate.

4th Evacuation Complete returned to Dover.

A T. Cook Lieut RNR C.O.

*Lieutenant. Alfred Thomas Cook was the Commanding Officer of HMS **Medway Queen** - courtesy of Mrs. P. Kennedy.*

After Operation Dynamo, Lieutenant Cook, along with other Commanding Officers, was asked to nominate crew members whose efforts deserved recognition. He wrote to Vice Admiral Dover with his list on 20th June 1940 and sent in a supplementary list the following day. There was some duplication in the two lists and I have merged them into one for ease of reading. I have also omitted home addresses. The "T124 Articles" mentioned are the Navy contract under which civilian or RN Auxiliary personnel served on warships under Royal Navy control and discipline.

To Vice Admiral Dover

Your 1055 re evacuation from Dunkirk

The following officers and men are respectfully submitted for some recognition for endurance, initiative and good service manning boats to and from beach and general assistance under trying conditions.

Lieut Leonard Jolly RNVR (Navigating Officer). This officer worked himself to a standstill helping navigation of ship and bringing troops from shore until he collapsed on the 6th trip.

Sub Lieut John David Graves RNR (1st Lieut). This officer helped with boats from beach to ship. He stood up for the whole of the seven trips. Address unknown. Left ship to join HMS Vernon (Portsmouth) as trainer in minesweeping.

<u>Sub Lieut John Vernon Davies RNR</u> (Chief Engineer). This officer worked night and day until he collapsed on the 7th voyage.

<u>Sub Lieut T. Irvine RNR</u> (2nd Engineer). This officer did, after the Chief and 3rd Engineers had collapsed through exhaustion, carry on night and day for seven trips. Thereby getting the ship back to port on the 7th trip. He is submitted for special commendation.

<u>Sub Lieut G. Ranger RNR</u> (3rd Engineer). This officer did although of a weak constitution, go ashore under incessant shell fire for many trips for troops. He collapsed after the third voyage and he is now under medical care.

<u>Thomas Russell</u> (Cook T124 articles). This man kept up night and day cooking and supplying hot food and drinks to troops throughout the seven trips.

<u>Kenneth Roy Olley RNVR</u> (seaman) did exceptional service, helping wounded from beach and keeping the motor launch with a dud engine running, towing troops to ship, for the whole seven trips.

<u>John Develand Connell</u> (Fireman T124 articles). This man volunteered for the running of boats from the beach. He did good work all through helping wounded and running boats to beach. He stuck to his duties during the whole seven trips.

<u>Harry McAllister</u> (P.O.) This man continually went in charge of boats to beach under fire throughout the whole evacuation.

<u>Alfred Earnest Crossley RFR</u> (Coxswain P.O.) good service ashore under fire at Dunkirk organising parties of troops. He did good service for the whole seven trips.

Joseph Richard James RFR (Leading Seaman). This man brought down two enemy aircraft during period of evacuation. He, in the face of power dive attack, did not waver, but kept gun on enemy until brought down.

Arthur Leslie Harrison (Steward T124 articles) This man showed willingness and gave service night and day for the whole period serving army officers, troops, ship's officers and anybody with food and drink. He kept to his job.

A. T. Cook

Lieut. RNR

C.O.

The Admiralty accepted many of Lt. Cook's suggestions and added another:

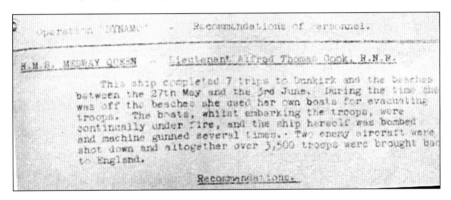

The above is a facsimile of the report from Lieutenant Cook, sadly it has faded over the years but reads as follows:

"This ship completed seven trips to Dunkirk and the beaches between the 27th May and the 3rd June. During the time she was off the beaches she used her own boats for evacuating troops. The boats, whilst embarking troops, were continually under fire, and the ship herself was bombed and machine gunned several times. Two enemy aircraft were shot down and altogether over 3,500 troops were brought back to England."

HER FINEST HOUR
Lt. John David Graves RNVR

All ships acquire a personality and sometimes this is so strong as to become evident even to strangers. Such a ship is *Medway Queen*.

I had not seen her since 1940 and I came across her lying tranquilly in a mud berth on the Medina river, Isle of Wight, on the evening that I had the honour of declaring her open as "name ship and club" of a yacht marina. When I went aboard her I felt exactly the same manifestation of her personality that I had known twenty five years before. Carpets and cocktail bars had taken the place of the guns and grey paint she had worn when last we met, but the feeling was the same. Here was a clean, efficient and cheerful little ship, anxious to do her work, and do it well.

For me, it all started in October 1939 when, as a young sub-lieutenant in the Royal Naval Reserve, and rising 21, I was appointed as her First Lieutenant, the Navy's name for second in command and my first job was to commission her.

I found *Medway Queen* lying in Deptford Creek undergoing refitting as a minesweeper (of moored mines - the only type in use at that time). She looked very small, very dirty and quite inadequate to her task, as somehow ships always do in dockyard. As work proceeded, however, she assumed an increasingly belligerent air. Uniform grey paint transformed the black hull and white upper works. Her bridge was enlarged and strengthened, minesweeping davits, floats and kites were fitted aft. A 12 pounder gun which first saw service in Flanders in 1915 was planted in her bows and machine gun posts were rigged on either sponson. Internally the plush fittings, tables and tea urns so recently in use by happy holiday

Opposite top: Sub-Lieutenant John David Graves RNVR (right) with two other officers - courtesy of PSPS Collection.

*Opposite bottom: "Watching the sweeps on HMS **Medway Queen**" - courtesy of PSPS Collection.*

*Right: Fo'c'sle and bridge of HMS **Medway Queen** in 1940 - courtesy of PSPS Collection.*

crowds were stripped out and severely practical mess decks fitted in their place, ready to receive a naval crew.

In about the middle of November the crew arrived and we lost no time in commissioning HMS *Medway Queen*. Our ship's company represented almost all the classes being mobilised for the Navy in war. As for the officers, it is a curious fact that our ranks were exactly reversed. Thus the Captain*, a paddle minesweeping veteran of the First World War and a Merchant Service Master of no mean experience as well, was a sub-lieutenant RNVR. Next there was myself, also with one ring, but RNR and hence just that bit senior to my Captain. Thirdly we had Lieutenant Jolly, RNVR, a peacetime yachtsman, and now our navigator - with two rings on his sleeve he was senior to both of us. Finally, Lieutenant Keily RNR, a tough old deep water sailorman, sixty six years young, had persuaded our Captain to sign him on as Junior Officer. This reversion of rank was typical of the disturbed state of minor naval affairs in those early days of the war, but it worked and it worked well. For a while *Medway Queen* swept the lower reaches of the Thames Estuary based in Harwich as a single ship attached to no particular flotilla and under the direct orders of the FOIC Harwich. This was the bitter winter of 1939, when even the estuary partly froze over, and for weeks on end a tug was required to go before us morning and night so that our paddles would not be damaged by the ice floes, which were sometimes quite large. The seas that came aboard froze, and decks and rails became coated with ice which had to be chipped away to restore stability. Day after day the little ship plunged out into the North Sea, streaming her sweeps and searching the depths, returning home each night with little to report except that the shipping channels were clear. The winter seas found many weaknesses in the hull and machinery of a ship which was then some

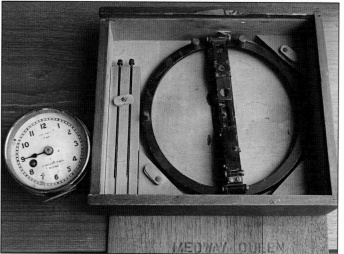

sixteen years old and used to summer sailings in protected waters, so in early December we were ordered to Chatham where the dockyard took over and the crew were given leave.

By then the men had become welded into a really efficient ship's company. Our

*Navigational instruments from HMS **Medway Queen**, probably from a ship's boat. Now on display at the Visitor Centre.*

Petty Officers and Leading Seamen were of that elite, the Royal Fleet Reserve. These were men who, after long years of Naval service, had retired but were retained on the register by Admiralty choice against recall in times of emergency. Thus we had Petty Officer Crossley, appointed Coxswain, the senior rating, and Petty Officer McAllister, a magnificent practical sailor who had been beneath the mines in the Dardanelles in the First War as a torpedo-man in a submarine. I designated him "Bo'sun of the Upper Deck" and in his charge we placed the training and welfare of the young conscript seamen who made up the bulk of the deck crew. In addition we had Leading Seamen Skinner and James, also RFR men of immense worth. It was, incidentally, surprising how the rather weedy young lads who came to us at the start of the commission filled out with hard work and plenty of food. I well remember in June 1940, when I left the ship, I was struck by the size of these same young men. They were keen because we made them so, and they were efficient: our Petty Officers and "Killicks"** saw to that.

When the Dockyard finished its work and the men returned from leave *Medway Queen* joined the 10th minesweeping flotilla in January 1940. This was as part of the Dover Patrol and was under the command of Commander Greig RN of HMS *Sandown*, a paddle steamer from the Isle of Wight. Our unusual minesweeping gear attracted much interest. We had discarded the lifeboat-type davits supplied to us for launching the floats and kites, in the absence of torpedo davits which were in short supply, and "found" (we became quite good at that) a tall Samson post and derrick in Chatham Dockyard which we carried aboard one night and, at the cost of a case of whisky, had welded to the after deck, abaft the mine-sweeping winch. This structure gave greater height and improved the handling of the heavy equipment so much that we had not been in the flotilla more than a week or two before every record for fast and efficient handling of the sweeping gear was in our possession and remained there.

"EEE", that is the Naval signal of

P.O. Henry McAllister who won the DSM at Dunkirk for his work with the boats bringing men from the beaches - courtesy of his son Dennis.

17

congratulation (Evolution Excellently Executed) with our pendants attached was often hoisted by the Senior Officer. Here we have the point of my story and the reason why *Medway Queen* excited so much interest when her sale for scrap looked like being a real possibility. Our crew were trained to do not only what was expected of them but to do it quicker, better, and more often than anyone else. That is why *Medway Queen* made seven trips to Dunkirk; seven nights of hell, and she never missed a trip. She would, I think, have made seventeen if the troops had been there to fill her.

And so it came about that, as part of the 10th flotilla, and by now appointed sub-divisional leader, *Medway Queen* swept the Straits of Dover while the nation slumbered and the German Army made ready to invade the Low Countries in the spring of 1940. She brought up her share of mines, she had her share of misfortune, but there were good times also and humour and incidents. Her crew thought as one and acted as one; any weaker members had been eliminated by the hard scope of her duties during that long and bitter winter. Machinery and paddles, though lacking the care and maintenance they deserved (a state common to the overworked Navy of those days) remained basically sound – a credit to her builders.

During the latter half of May 1940 it became the practice of the flotilla to anchor in various road-steads to act as mine-spotting craft (for mines laid from the air) after the day's work of sweeping was over. It was at such an anchorage on the 27th May 1940 that orders came to proceed to beaches north of Dunkirk and embark some troops who would be waiting there.

Eight ships weighed anchor that night comprising *Sandown, Gracie Fields, Queen of Thanet, Thames Queen, Princess Elizabeth, Laguna Belle, Brighton Belle* and *Medway Queen*. In line ahead they steamed through the night to a point about half a mile from the shore where, in the first faint light of dawn, could be made out long lines of men standing still like human piers stretching out into the water – knee, waist even neck high in it; standing so patiently there in full equipment; boots, rifles, packs, tin helmets and all, with sergeants passing or rather swirling their way up and down the lines with a word of encouragement here and a command there. Orders were to leave by daylight but in the face of what we found this was not possible and, as dawn broke, the ships put off their lifeboats to be rowed or towed to the heads of the human queues. So began what must have been the very start of the evacuation from the beaches at Dunkirk.

The anti-aircraft cruiser *Calcutta* stood by, giving support against any German aircraft which ventured over, but apart from a few bombs which went wide, there were no untoward incidents, and at 7:00 am *Medway Queen* with the rest of the flotilla left the beaches and headed for Dover***. On the way back and outside the harbour a heavy air raid developed during which *Medway Queen* shot down a German fighter. In the confusion *Brighton Belle* drifted over a submerged wreck, tore her bottom out and began to sink. We went alongside and took off her soldiers, together with her crew, before the old ship subsided to the bottom. We then continued on our way to Dover and disembarked the soldiers. They were mostly

Aft view of HMS **Medway Queen** *showing the minesweeping equipment - courtesy of PSPS Collection.*

base personnel, line of communications troops and AA gunners. One wonders who gave the latter priority in the evacuation – they were to be sorely missed at Dunkirk later.

The flotilla reassembled at 5:00pm that second day and once again, in line ahead, steamed out from Dover and made for Dunkirk, this time with instructions to enter the harbour. Off the entrance the flotilla came under very heavy fire from shore batteries, and some of the ships hauled out of the line as the sea spouted columns of water around them. The scene was awe-inspiring. Rows of great oil tanks were blazing furiously and the glare was reflected on the clouds. Heavy shells plunged into the harbour which was littered with wrecks. It was enough to daunt the stoutest navigator, but still the ships came and went, feeling their way past uncharted obstructions and avoiding each other. Our Captain, after consulting with his officers, decided we should act independently of the flotilla, make our way into Dunkirk, fill up with troops and leave. We had by then realised that there were

Troops wading out to the ships at Dunkirk. Taken from the bridge under difficult circumstances and in a rush - courtesy of PSPS Collection.

not just small pockets of soldiers to be lifted but virtually the whole British Expeditionary Force and part of the French and Belgian armies as well. The officers all agreed that the ship should go to and fro in her own time and continue to do so for as long as it was possible. The others evidently reached the same conclusion for the flotilla did not again sail as a unit. On the way in that second night the sea was unusually phosphorescent. Our paddles left broad twin wakes and on occasions German aircraft followed these wakes to their end and dropped bombs uncomfortably close. We were nothing if not resourceful aboard *Medway Queen* and devised oil bags which were lowered over the bow on either side just as they were used at sea to break the force of heavy waves. This was most successful, our brilliant wakes disappeared and *Medway Queen* went on her way in decent obscurity. Again, at the most critical point of the trip when we were creeping along the French coast past Gravelines, the funnel began to stream sparks, caused by deposited soot catching fire. We were cross with the Chief Engineer of course but there was nothing he could do about it. However, those sparks made the ship a very obvious target and they had to be suppressed. There followed a hilarious half hour, set against the tragic background of burning Dunkirk. A bucket chain was formed from the main deck and up the ladders to that part of the flying bridge which approached the funnel. Our tallest sailor took the buckets of water and tried to tip their contents down the funnel to put out the fire or at least to damp it down. This was reasonably successful but not much appreciated by the engine room staff. At one stage a voice from the gloomy depths of the funnel insisted that he did not intend to be "blank" well drowned on the job!

The harbour that night presented the appearance, to become all too familiar, of the wreck of one of the most modern ports in Europe. Docks and quay walls were rubble, and torn and broken ships lay everywhere. One single pier remained, the outer mole on the north side of the harbour. Never designed for handling goods or allowing the passage of men, it was all that was left, and the Navy decided to use it. It can be said of that concrete strip that it helped save Britain and the free world. Along its length walked, stumbled or were carried very nearly a quarter of a million men during the nine days of the evacuation. Ships were sunk alongside it, putting parts out of use. Lengths of it were torn away by shell or bomb. The gaps were repaired by mess tables from ships, by ladders, wood planking and other material taken from the debris around the harbour and all the time, silhouetted by flames at night and looking drawn and tired by day, the weary file of men stumbled along its length.

Many types of ship made fast to that mole. Destroyers, with their advantages of speed and manoeuvrability, played a significant part but there were also the personnel carriers as the pre-war cross channel ships were described, and the hospital ships, the trawlers, the drifters, the Dutch Skoots - every variety of small ship, civilian and naval, and of course the paddle minesweepers. All in their turn, filled up and went, and let it be said there was never any distinction between nationalities or services. All who came were taken. Any man who presented himself abreast the ship was embarked. Only civilian families were excluded. The

Evacuated troops on board HMS Medway Queen - courtesy of PSPS Collection.

rule was firmly enforced. These were hard times and had it become known that transport to Britain was available, crowds of refugees might have turned up to their own great danger and the exclusion of men needed to defend our island. Priority had to be given to fighting soldiers.

As the days came and went the drill became familiar. Once alongside scaling ladders were erected as the height of the mole was much above the decks of *Medway Queen*. Some of the crew went ashore to control and direct the soldiers, to assist the wounded and so on. Work went on to an accompaniment of rough oaths and crude instructions, hurrying and harrying, but in the exhausted state of most of the soldiers it proved to be the right approach. It went on against a background of blazing oil tanks, the scream, splash and explosion of shells, the roar of bombs and heavy detonations from the city where demolition was proceeding. Finally, when the old ship was down nearly to her sponsons in the water, the word would come to the Captain "We're full up, Sir - time we went" and freeing ourselves from the berth we'd make our way down the fairway and out into the roads with Lieutenant Jolly navigating - and no better navigator ever conned a ship.

Once clear of the harbour we would pick our way through the cleared channels, known as X and Y, or on occasion if the tide was right slip over the minefields to save time, relying on our shallow draft to get us by. After the first day we used Ramsgate as it was less congested than Dover. We would arrive back at about 10 or 11 in the morning, disembark our troops, take on oil, fuel, water and stores, or whatever stores were available, and proceed out to the roadstead to await dusk and our next trip. Some nights we were directed to the harbour at Dunkirk, sometimes diverted to the beaches, but as day followed night and night followed day without respite weariness blurred the outline of events. Only the habit of discipline and the power of men's wills kept our little ship to her appointed task.

At the beaches a different drill applied. As soon as we dropped anchor the boats were lowered, manned and towed away by the motor dinghy to the beaches where the soldiers waited so patiently in the water. When the boats returned we hauled the soldiers aboard by the sponson doors behind the paddle boxes, and away the boats went for another quota of human cargo - and so on through the night until with the approaching dawn we sailed for home.

Mistakes occurred of course. One very dark night we waited long hours with neither sight nor sound of our boats. The Captain was getting worried and very angry. Finally, near dawn, the motor dinghy arrived with two loaded cutters in tow, drew alongside with a flourish and a cheerful voice called out "That should just about fill you, Sir". "What do you so-and-so mean?" roared the Captain. "This is the first load we've seen all night!" We used a private signal on our blue signal lamp for the boats to home on. Evidently someone else had chanced to adopt our signal and, in the darkness our boats had obligingly filled up another paddler! We had perforce to delay while the boats made several more runs before we could decently up anchor and return to Britain.

Now, I would like you to picture *Medway Queen* on any one of those crossings. Let us start forward in the windlass flat, directly below the fo'c'sle head. Here we had had the "cells". As was perhaps inevitable, we collected a few undesirables - drunks, suspicious characters and suspected fifth columnists among the thousands we took on board. Here we deposited them under the watchful eye of Stoker Jackson, our self-appointed jailer, until they could be handed over to the authorities at Ramsgate.

Coming aft, on the port side, was the Petty Officers' mess, converted for the evacuation to a sick bay where wounded or dying soldiers were placed under the care of our sick bay rating. With very little equipment or supplies he did his best to ease their pains or their passing. One young soldier, badly wounded asked to be lifted up to see the white cliffs of England as we approached - and died in my arms as I raised him towards a porthole.

On the starboard side was the stokers' mess, where our merchant service firemen lived. Below, and reached by a companionway, was the seamen's mess filling the width of the ship. All the bunks and most of the floor space here, as in the stokers' mess also, was given over to soldiers, often leaving the crew with nowhere to lay their heads in rare off-duty hours.

Next came the galley where the cook, a tall quiet individual, toiled night and day to prepare for and feed the never ending line of hungry mouths that passed his doors. It was one of our boasts that every soldier who came aboard was fed, and with one assistant only, he never let them down. Immediately aft of the galley came the engine room space, separated by rails from the alleyways on either side but otherwise open to view, with the control platform at its rear, overlooking the machinery. Here, Chief Engineer Davis, *Medway Queen*'s engineer in peacetime, tended the levers and wheels with which he controlled the engine and rotation of the paddles. In confined waters and under attack the safety of the ship depended on the promptness with which the engineer followed orders from the bridge relayed to him by the engine room telegraph. Throughout the evacuation Engineer Davis, like the Captain, never left his station while the ship was at sea. By the time it was all over he was grey with strain and weariness.

Once I recall a man in soldier's uniform - perhaps ill disposed, perhaps a little "round the bend" from the experiences he had survived - was leaning over the engine room rail fingering the pin of a grenade. It was very smartly removed from him by those around and he was hustled away to Stoker Jackson to be locked up until he could be handed over to the Military Police at Ramsgate.

Still going aft, behind the engine room, the main companionway led up to the decks. The stern was occupied by the officers' living quarters with stores below. The wardroom (mess) was made over to army officers during the returns from Dunkirk. They crowded every available space, stripping off wet clothes, stretched out asleep, having a meal or just talking - endlessly discussing how and why this humiliating retreat had overtaken an army which had not been beaten in the field. The stewards laboured in the wardroom, as did the ship's cook forward, to supply food to all who needed it and won much appreciation for their efforts.

Every alleyway was choked with troops, stretched out exhausted or else jostling, talking, arguing and so on. The decks also were crowded with soldiers. On the weather deck the 12 pounder was always manned, as were the Lewis guns on the sponsons, and these were always attended by volunteer groups of soldiers to fill the magazines and thereby feel they were "having a crack" at Jerry. On about the third trip there appeared a sand-bagged enclosure on the after deck, set up by three army cadets - stout lads, none over twenty - who wanted to come aboard, bringing with them 2 Bren guns, which they then manned to excellent effect throughout the remainder of the evacuation. On *Medway Queen* we believed in concentrated firepower. I took a party ashore at Dunkirk and succeeded in "borrowing" a number of abandoned Bren guns, these were lashed to stays and shrouds with a single turn of rope which formed an ideal swivel. Provided with a pile of ammunition beside each, they were handy for whoever was nearest to use in an attack. Beyond this, all troops and sailors who had a rifle were encouraged to blaze away at approaching aircraft on the principle that a storm of rifle fire could be as effective as a number of machine guns. The total result was impressive in discouraging any close approach by hostile aircraft and certainly contributed to *Medway Queen*'s survival and our good score of three low flying aircraft shot down during the evacuation.

Many curious happenings occurred - there was the party of Spanish sailors, refugees from an earlier war, caught in France by the German advance whom we picked up from a raft at sea. They spoke little English but settled down happily. It happened that night that we were hailed in English by a naval officer in a small motor vessel with instructions to proceed twelve miles up the coast where a pocket of troops had been cut off and were awaiting evacuation. We set off, but speaking by chance to the Spaniards, they were horrified and gave us to understand the place had been in German hands for two days. They had escaped from there! Later we heard it said that a destroyer had been similarly hailed that night and torpedoed when it hove to, but that another destroyer, aware of this, when also hailed, had opened fire and sunk the motor vessel. There was every opportunity for fifth columnists to infiltrate in the chaos in and around Dunkirk, and there is no doubt that some did. A few, fortunately very few, E boats (motor torpedo craft) slipped through the naval screen under cover of darkness to add to the hazards of shell and bomb which we had to face.

Lieutenant Charles Keily - courtesy of the Keily family.

Our abortive trip delayed arrival at the beaches and with the coming of daylight enemy activity further delayed loading, and we were hours late getting back to Ramsgate. We had been posted missing but only learned of this the following day when papers came aboard and we read that, "after-all *Medway Queen* had returned safely".

By Monday, June 3rd, the Germans were finally closing in on Dunkirk. At mid-day Vice Admiral Ramsay issued orders that all ships were to leave Dunkirk by 2:30 the following morning. *Medway Queen* set out on her 7th trip - thereby establishing a record for all ships below the size of destroyer. We berthed beside the mole for the last time at midnight, and machine gun fire could be clearly heard. The sands were running out very fast. We took on board about 400 French troops - all the BEF had by this time left (in the final stages the French held the shrinking perimeter). Shelling in the harbour was very heavy. A destroyer astern of *Medway Queen* was hit and flung forward against our starboard paddle box, extensively damaging the sponson. About 1:00am our Captain nursed us clear of the berth, with difficulty, because of the damaged sponson, and *Medway Queen* made off very slowly down the harbour under the sure hands of Lieutenant Jolly, with the familiar mole, still lit by blazing oil tanks, falling astern, and Lieutenant Keily strumming a mandolin on the after deck to cheer up the tired Frenchmen****.

Among the first to arrive off the beaches, *Medway Queen* was one of the last to leave Dunkirk on the morning of Tuesday June 4th 1940 and damaged, worn out and very weary we limped into Dover. The evacuation had ended. Vice Admiral Ramsay signalled "Well Done *Medway Queen*" and the ships in harbour sounded their sirens as we made for our buoys. This was a very proud moment.

First published by PSPS in 1974 and reproduced with permission of PSPS and Susan Murray, Lt. Graves' daughter.

* Sub-Lieutenant R D C Cooke RNVR, who was HMS *Medway Queen*'s Captain from commissioning until shortly before Dunkirk. His replacement, Lt. A. T. Cook RNR, assumed command on 20th May 1940.

** Leading Seamen.

*** The log kept for *Medway Queen*, although typed up at a later date, states that they off loaded the troops at Ramsgate on this, and most subsequent, trips.

**** Charles Keily's granddaughter, Gillie Richardson, remembers meeting Basil Barendt after the war, at a school where he was teaching. He had been rescued from Dunkirk by HMS *Medway Queen* and remembered a mandolin session on the voyage back. Gillie thinks Charles' musical performances were not limited to the last trip.

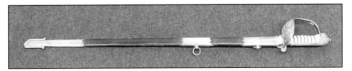

Sub-Lieutenant Graves' dress sword.

25

*Loading stores on HMS **Medway Queen**, bound for Dunkirk - courtesy of MQPS Collection.*

Dunkirk beach - courtesy of PSPS Collection.

"GO TO THE GALLEY DOOR, BOYS"

Thomas Russell

I swayed on sore feet, my head ached abominably and my body was racked with fatigue as up until then I had had no sleep for 72 hours. The month of May 1940 was waning and the wartime evacuation from Dunkirk - the greatest evacuation in military history - was in full swing. It was 4am.

The end of a bandage was dipping in the mess-tin that was held out to me but I was unable to stop my robot-like dip and pour rhythm in time to avoid emptying a ladle of stew over it. Curiosity made me look up and some drops of perspiration fell from the end of my nose into the stew. The soldier I saw was wounded in the head, his young face pinched and white under the blood-soaked field dressing. Blood and sweat. They were certainly fitting symbols of the harrowing event we were experiencing and the manner of its achievement I thought. Our eyes met as, reaching out, he removed the bandage then heartily sucked the gravy from the end of it before tucking the end of it back in place. It was a strange gesture and I wondered when he had eaten last. He grinned at me as if it hurt his lips to stretch them. "Thanks Pal. Tastes smashing!"

I returned the smile wanly and hoped it conveyed to him not to mention it; that it was my pleasure. However, he was only one of the seemingly endless queue of men who were clamouring for food and there was soon another mess tin waiting to be filled. And another, and another. Would the nightmare never end?

When the evacuation was over the small paddle steamer converted into a minesweeper in which I was serving as Chief Cook had carved her name in the annals of naval wartime history by making more trips to the beaches of Dunkirk than any other vessel except the fast destroyers. It was an unbroken week of nightly visits with the German Luftwaffe and shore batteries seeking her out as a special target - a menace - as the evacuation progressed. This was not surprising as she alone brought safely back to England as many as 7,000 servicemen.

Immediately they were marshalled aboard these troops were invited by our crew to go to the galley if they were hungry or thirsty. IF! Most of those 7,000 men accepted the invitation during the nights that followed. Not one left the galley empty handed. I had one young assistant cook nicknamed "Sec".*

It all began on the last Sunday in May. The paddle steamer was the *Medway Queen* of the 10th flotilla of minesweepers attached to the Dover Patrol. It was mid-morning and she was riding at anchor in the shadows of Dover's white cliffs. Sec and I were leaning on the rail enjoying a mug of tea in the early summer breeze before continuing preparations for lunch for the crew of 48 the sweeper carried. It was an extraordinary day and we wondered what was up.

In the first place we could not make out why none of the flotilla were out on the usual daily sweep. Indeed the whole 10th flotilla seemed to have foregathered at Dover. We recognised *Brighton Belle*, *Thames Queen*, *Queen of Thanet*, *Gracie Fields*; all paddle steamers though like *Medway Queen* each was painted battleship grey and only showed a number. Also, immediately after breakfast a launch had toured the flotilla and every captain, First Officer and wireless operator was now on the flagship engaged in a mysterious conference. And now a naval barge had finished unloading into our little craft a tremendous amount of food supplies - every storage space was crammed and crates and boxes spilled out onto the alleyways near the galley. We watched the barge as it pulled away. Sec's remark was innocently prophetic: "Enough grub's been put on board us to feed a ruddy army" he said.

The next day the news filtered through to us. Paris had fallen** and our lads were retreating under orders to the Dunkirk beaches. The whole flotilla was going to move out together at dusk to bring back to England as many of them as they could. My orders from Captain Cook came at about 5pm on Monday, May 27th, and were to use the stores that were put on board as I thought best and to prepare hot food, sandwiches and drinks for "several hundred men who will no doubt feel somewhat peckish". So immediately we had cleared dinner out of the way - about 7pm - Sec and I each took a quick shower and returned to the galley. We knew we were in for a long hot session and were wearing only singlets with our whites.

The galley of *Medway Queen*, principally used in peacetime for preparing light refreshments and the fish and chip teas so beloved by cockney trippers, was not large. It wasn't an easy job merely to cook three square meals a day for our crew. It contained, along with the sink, workbenches and cupboards, a temperamental and hungry coal range that took up a third of the space. There certainly wasn't much room for moving about and Sec and I had become adept at working together without bumping into each other. The galley lay athwartships on the middle deck with a divided door at port and starboard, each facing an alley-way. I butchered a carcass of mutton and then proceeded to prepare carrots, onions and potatoes - countless sacks of them - to make an Irish stew using all the largest pots I had. Sec had the task of cutting up dozens of loaves (we had no convenient sliced, wrapped bread in those days) and make as many sandwiches as he could using cheeses and tinned meats. We made several pots full of Navy Cocoa, opened a dozen or so tins of condensed milk into each one and put water on to boil in our several large iron kettles, ready to make tea or coffee. We worked on at a steady pace, undisturbed except by the steward and his bottomless coffee pot.

It wasn't until every space on the stove was covered with steaming pans and we had a "mountain" of sandwiches made that we noticed the time. It was 2:30am. Our singlets were wringing wet. We were very tired. We had been too busy to pay much attention to anything going on outside the galley, but now we were acutely aware of the noises - of the whistling of the shells - the crack of explosions - of our ship's guns blasting away. I relaxed for a moment on the folding stool I kept in the galley and rolled a cigarette. Sec wandered outside for some air. He was back in a flash.

"Chief", his young voice squeaked with excitement, "Come and see!". Wearily I prised myself loose and went up on deck with him. The ship was anchored in the deep channel outside Dunkirk Harbour and all of the crew not immediately occupied were also there - transfixed - standing on the blacked-out ship, in silhouette one moment then reflected in the flashes of bombs and gunfire the next. Everyone seemed awestricken, and no wonder.

The scene, which has been immortalised in books and on film - was one to which we returned six further times and I shall never forget it. The unexpected sight of every British craft imaginable from single rowing boats to destroyers which rallied to Dunkirk at that time - the fierce opposition from the enemy. Mixed emotions of fear - horror - wonder and pride fought for supremacy inside me as I gazed about, swallowing a huge lump in my throat. Mixed up in the inferno were our boys - hundreds and hundreds of them - patiently waiting in queues. Many were up to their necks in the water. They were being machine gunned by swooping 'planes as we watched, many falling never to rise again. Presently, I realised that the launch heading our way which held about 60 soldiers would soon be alongside us. Sec came running up to me. "I've just heard we are taking a thousand if we can!" A thousand! This was the ship's full passenger capacity in peacetime. I felt panic starting to engulf me. We'll never cope, I thought. Oh God - we haven't got nearly enough food prepared. We flew back to the galley, opening tins of beans, tins of milk and making pots of tea. We could hardly move about, the galley was so full of food, but much more would be needed. How we were going to serve - and keep a stream of it coming - I just could not foresee.

Suddenly there was a crush at each galley door, with innumerable khaki clad arms - many dripping wet - waving billy-cans, mugs and mess tins at us. The hubbub was clamorous and insistent. These weren't "peckish" men. These were starving animals, most of them too desperately hungry and thirsty to be polite - pushing, shoving and shouting. Someone opened the starboard half door and they started to flood for service right into the galley, then tried to exit through the other door. Sec and I were serving as fast as we could but we were getting shoved back and forth and could scarcely manage. Some of the lads started to help themselves, it was pandemonium.

I pushed through the crush and pulled at the sleeve of the first ship's officer I saw (to this day I cannot remember whose arm was in it). He was very calm and efficient, and soon had the whole thing organised, with the lads forming orderly queues for service at both doors. Sec and I were working like machines, handing out sustenance to our desperate compatriots in a never ending stream. We ran out of stew nearly half-way back and as the ship was nosing into Ramsgate Harbour at about 7:30am - which harbour was to be our home base during the operation - we had served great quantities of baked beans, sausages, eggs, chops - anything we could lay our hands on and pop on the range and into the ovens.

When the last of the troops had left there was no time in which to relax. We not only had to prepare the normal meals during the day for our crew but also had to start preparation for the coming night. The "*Queen*" wasn't going to go out sweeping until the evacuation was completed but the mammoth clearing up operation kept all hands hard at work. Mud and sand were everywhere - countless abandoned rifles and items of kit - empty cigarette packets, bottles and paper by the cartload - it seemed as if hundreds of the men had been seasick. There was

Dunkirk harbour - courtesy of PSPS Collection.

hardly an inch of the ship that didn't require to be washed down.

My responsibility weighed heavily upon me, as I knew I was the only person on the ship with the necessary experience to cook in quantity. Sec's help was needed - and invaluable - but he was only a lad in his teens and inexperienced. It was up to me to see that there was plenty of tasty hot food.

And so there commenced what was to become a marathon of human endurance, not just for Sec and me but for every member of the crew from Captain Cook and First Officer Graves to the youngest AB. During the days the formidable cleaning-up job and preparation for the following night. During the nights our thousand weary, war-torn, hungry guests to collect and care for during the fight to bring them home under incessant bombardment. To this day I do not know how we managed to keep upright and to carry on working.

I know that somehow I managed to keep awake during that week of horror - by snatching mini-sleeps during short periods of lull, sitting upright on my galley stool - by grabbing every opportunity that presented itself to take a cold shower - by drinking innumerable cups of strong tea and black coffee liberally laced with spirit.

The days merged and became like one. Torpor took over. My actions became automatic. My movements became jerky. My attitude to others became anti-social. There were periods of near delirium when I was haunted by visions of satin-cool cushions on which to rest my head - and my feet, but before I could reach them

The Medway Queen Club in 1971, Bob Tebbutt - courtesy of Chris Tebbutt.

they turned into sandwiches and mess-tins of stew being grabbed away by dozens of grubby, disembodied hands.

At dawn on June 4th the last muddy, ragged, Khaki-clad figure - not nearly so hungry and thirsty as when he'd arrived - left Medway Queen and a three day recuperative leave was given to all of the crew. I could not concentrate to pack and stretched out. I was the only human being left in the "Queen". She and I - bless her - were both glad it was over and I'm sure I heard her tired struts creaking as did my bones, as we both settled down to our well-earned rest. Undisturbed, I slept the clock round and then I went home and slept some more.

In 1966 with my brother and our wives we celebrated our retirement after 40 years of seafaring by dining once more in the Medway Queen. This time I enjoyed a superb meal in leisurely, luxurious style. Due for scrapping, Medway Queen was purchased by an enterprising group of young business men on the Isle of Wight. She was now a very beautiful lady indeed, with first class amenities for dining, wining and dancing. She was still a paddle steamer but moored by the shore of the river Medina near Cowes. My galley was a storage cupboard. She carried a brass plaque commemorating her great effort during those historic days and it was with a deep feeling of pride, when asked to sign her visitors' book, that I saw carefully added in red letters beside my name "Ships Cook during Dunkirk".

First published by PSPS in 1974 and reproduced with permission of PSPS.
* We now know that "Sec" was Stanley Bell.
** The rumour was not quite true. Paris was not occupied until June 14th.

A list of members of HMS *Medway Queen*'s Dunkirk crew that are known to the Society

Bell, Stanley	Assistant Cook
Campbell, Jock	Seaman
Connell, John Develand	Fireman (T124 articles)
Consadine, Philip Stanley	Stoker
Cook Alfred Thomas	Lieut. RNR, Commanding Officer
Crossley, Alfred Earnest	Petty Officer, Coxswain
Davis (or Davies), John Vernon	Chief Engineer
Day, Jim	Seaman
Feathers, Jack	RASC Officer Cadet Volunteer
Graves John David	Sub Lieut. RNR, First Lieutenant
Greig, K. M.	Acting Cdr. HMS Sandown
Harrison, Arthur Leslie	Steward (T124 articles)
Imthurn (or Im Thurn), John	RASC Officer Cadet Volunteer
Irvine, Thomas	Sub Lieut. RNR 2nd Engineer
Jackson	Stoker
James, Joseph Richard (Jimmy)	Leading Seaman RFR
Jolly, Leonard	Lieut. RNVR Navigating officer
Keily, Charles	Lieut. RNR, Junior Officer
Keytes, Bill	Seaman
Lewis	Seaman
Maraga, Arthur	Seaman
Mathias, William	Trainee telegraphist
Matthews, Roger	Seaman
McAllister, Harry J.	Petty Officer, Bo'sun
Nason, Albert	Seaman
Olley, Kenneth Roy	Seaman
Penman, Norman	Army Volunteer
Perry, Yorkie	Seaman
Ranger, G.	Sub Lieut. RNR 3rd Engineer
Rayment, Brian	RASC Officer Cadet Volunteer
Russell, Thomas	Ship's Cook (T124 articles)
Skinner, Albert J	Leading Seaman RFR
Skinner, Jack	Seaman
Spot	Ship's dog
Sutton, Bruce	Seaman
Walker, Charlie	Seaman
Woodroffe, Eric	Signalman
Unknown, Robbie	Seaman

THE DUNKIRK CREW'S MEMORIES

Thomas Irvine

From Full Ahead, Autumn 2017.

Two of *Medway Queen*'s crew were mentioned in despatches for their part in Operation Dynamo: Fireman John Connell and Second Engineer Thomas Irvine. Both awards were announced, together, in the London Gazette for 16th August 1940. Seonaid Boyle kindly contacted the society, asking if we would be interested in adding Thomas Irvine's "mentioned in despatches" certificate to our collection and archive. Only one possible answer of course! Not only has Seonaid donated the certificate (below) but also this photograph of Thomas from his time in the Royal Navy and a copy of the London Gazette entry for his award. Thomas' connection with Seonaid's family is something of a mystery which we are unlikely to solve - unless one of you knows better… !

Photo and certificate courtesy of Seonaid Boyle

The Gazette is in fact available on line in searchable form. A few minutes at the keyboard turned up the entries for other members of HMS *Medway Queen*'s crew who were decorated at the same time; all announced in the same issue. We already knew of these awards but it is always good to find further documentary evidence.

If you want to look yourself, allow for the fact that text searches on scanned PDF documents are not 100% reliable and that each search shows only the first instance of the text on each page.

The Lords Commissioners of the Admiralty hereby certify that
by the KING'S order the name of
Second Engineer Thomas Irvine,
H.M.S. Medway Queen,
was published in the London Gazette on
16 August, 1940,
as mentioned in Despatches for good service of which His Majesty's high appreciation is thus recorded.

Eric Woodroffe
From Full Ahead, Spring 2009.

Eric Woodroffe was a young signalman at the time of Dunkirk serving on HMS *Medway Queen*. Eric's story appeared in the MQPS magazine, Full Ahead, in spring 2009, written up by Kathie Clark who was society secretary at that time.

After a welcome leave, I was ordered to Chatham Dockyard to join HMS *Medway Queen* as signalman. I found her, both in name and appearance, even more unlike the usual idea of a warship than "*Blackfly*"*. *Medway Queen* was a paddle steamer which in peacetime had transported day-trippers between Herne Bay and Southend. She had been converted for minesweeping and was due to join a flotilla of similar craft at Dover. There were five paddle steamers in the flotilla: "*Sandown*" and "*Ryde*"** were former Southern Railway steamers plying to and from the Isle of Wight, while "*Brighton Belle*" and "*Gracie Fields*" had carried holiday makers on trips from the piers of south coast resorts. Dover was a huge improvement on Grimsby. Not only did it have pleasant cafes and cinemas but there was a good train service to London which made it possible to make a quick visit home when, on rare occasions, we had 48 hours' leave.

The Germans had laid a large minefield to the east of the Straits of Dover stretching across to the Dutch and Belgian coasts, and our flotilla was given the task of clearing it. Minesweeping can be done only in daylight and we used to anchor in the Downs, off Deal, each night. With the lengthening days of April and May this meant weighing anchor about 4.40am and returning about 9pm. We swept up many mines and were occasionally attacked by aircraft; the amount of communication necessary among the ships meant that I was almost continuously on duty - 1 was the only signalman on the ship. During the first few days of our minesweeping we began to receive news of the German advance through Belgium and Holland. Several times we came across fishing boats and even rowing boats packed with refugees; they were cold, wet, frightened and seasick. Some were ill or wounded; many women had small children and some of these children were dead. We did what we could for them and one ship in the flotilla would be detailed to take them back to Dover or Ramsgate. It was a stressful time and we were glad when we were at last able to return to Dover for a few days' leave. However, we were soon to find out what it was really like to be thoroughly tired and exhausted.

In the last week of May we received orders to steam at full speed for La Panne, east of Dunkirk, and evacuate troops from the beaches. Operation Dynamo, the evacuation of the British Army from Dunkirk had begun. We steamed through the night, guided by the flames of the burning buildings in Dunkirk. The paddle steamers were in great demand because their shallow draught enabled them to cross sand bars and go further inshore than most other craft.

As we approached the shore we could see queues of soldiers standing in the water and on the beach waiting patiently for rescue; behind them rows of wounded were laid out on the sand. Several times German planes came over and dropped bombs among them, but the soldiers said that the bombs buried themselves in the soft sand and did little damage. When they aimed for the ships it was much more serious and several destroyers and small craft were sunk. We and the other ships were also attacked on the way over and on the way back and many soldiers who thought they had been rescued and were now safe never reached home. One great blessing was that there was fog for a great deal of the time, and this gave us some concealment from aircraft. But for that the whole of the operation might have been impossible. Over the nine days (eight nights) we made seven trips - only one other ship, I believe, made more; four times to the open beaches and three times into Dunkirk harbour to embark directly from the ruined jetties. Half way through we were allowed to anchor off Ramsgate for twelve hours and have a good sleep. Apart from this we had no sleep and very little hot food over the nine days. Whether crossing the channel, embarking troops or disembarking at Dover or Ramsgate there was the ever-present threat, and often the reality, of air attack. Before the end we were so tired that we could hardly stand and some members of the crew, particularly those in the engine room, collapsed from exhaustion.

But there was an amazing spirit of determination, almost of exhilaration, unlike anything I have ever met before or since, which drove us to keep going. We knew that this was a national crisis. We knew that unless we got the army home our country would certainly be invaded and probably defeated. There was a feeling that we were in the middle of great events which would compare in history with the defeat of the Armada.

The evacuation of the army from Dunkirk has now become a legend; a saga of amateur sailors who left their work to take their yachts and motor boats over the channel to rescue an army. Many did this, and all honour to them, because it was a bloody business. But we must distinguish between the reality and the myth. It must not be forgotten that the majority of those who were rescued - about eighty five percent, I believe - came home in the warships of the Royal Navy. After it was all over and I had enjoyed a week's leave, I returned to Dover and learned that the flotilla was to be dispersed. We had lost two ships out of five and Dover, now under continual air attack and shell fire, was no place for a base. *Medway Queen* was ordered to North Shields on the Tyne. Here our task was to go out daily to sweep for mines in the approach channels to the Tyne and the port of Blyth and part of the main East Coast convoy channel. Planes were believed to be dropping mines at night. I don't know whether any were laid but during the summer and early autumn of 1940 I do not recall finding any. We did, however, have the occasional hit-and-run air attack.

*HMS *Blackfly* was an anti-submarine trawler, requisitioned in August 1939.
**HMS *Ryde* did join the flotilla but not until a few days after Dunkirk.

Albert Skinner

From his own account of his time in HMS Medway Queen.

Albert Skinner was 44 years old at the start of the war. He had served in the Royal Navy in the 1914-18 war and joined up again when the age limit for experienced men was raised to 45. He thinks he must have been the first man to take off a boat load of soldiers from the Dunkirk beaches.

The evacuation proper started on Monday night (for the moment I have forgotten the exact date) but the night before a member of the crew of a motor launch came aboard and told us there was a big operation coming off. They had been across to get the "lie of the land". On the way out we could see plenty of fire and hear the gun fire but at that time it was fairly well inland, but before the week was out I was right in amongst it in Dunkirk Harbour. The *Medway Queen* lay off the beaches and I took charge of a boat. Having two men with me - the soldiers would be manning the oars on the way back. I was instructed to make for a torch light and that other boats would be following later. I recollect an incident as I climbed down into the boat. One of the men, a leading seaman, a namesake of mine (there were three Skinners on board *Medway Queen* but we were not related), called down and asked me if I had any money in my belt, so I said I thought I had about three or four pounds, and he remarked that I had better let him have it in case they didn't see me anymore, and that if he was still in the land of the living he would send it on to the Mrs. (but fate decided that I should experience a good deal more before the end of the war).

I must say that at the outset (our first trip to Dunkirk) it was chaos complete, but the next time we went over it was a little better organised. I certainly had my work cut out governing the manning of the boat and used some pretty strong language, threatening to hit their hands with the tiller if they didn't let go of the boat when I was already well over-loaded. To make matters worse one of the soldiers shoved his rifle into my mouth and of course that made the air bluer than ever. I have still got the scar on my lip where he opened it up. It was certainly a bit of a job trying to stop the blood from my mouth and at the same time control this boatload. When I got back alongside the *Medway Queen* they shouted down asking me what I had been doing as my face had plenty of blood on it, but I said that it wasn't what I had done but what that so-and-so who's just coming aboard had done. Each time on the way back to the beach we had to bail out with our tin helmets. As the soldiers were up to their waists in water coming to the boat and they drained off on the way over. What I did take particular notice of was that not one of the soldiers had let go their rifles, except in the case of a blinded man and his rifle was carried by one of the men.

The *Medway Queen* certainly had a charmed life on those trips. I think it was on the fourth trip over that we went into Dunkirk Harbour and tied up alongside the jetty. We had taken a lot of troops on when a naval officer (Commander Buchannan) who was organising the troops called out to our skipper not to take any more because he wanted to have a merchant ship which was lying astern of us filled up first. Just after that a destroyer cut our stern rope and parted it, and the stern drifted out. There was a man aft and one for'ard with a butcher's cleaver in case we had to cut the mooring ropes away suddenly. Our captain shouted to us to chop the head rope and let it all go, including the brow (ship's gangway), and we drifted out towards the centre of the harbour. There was a big merchant packet bearing down on us, and I was so certain that it would hit us properly that I said to my mate "This is it, Fred, I stand a better chance with my sea boots off than on" and started to take them off, but fortunately it was a glancing blow and we just had a bit of a shake-up and righted ourselves. It was certainly a shambles in the harbour but flames were supplying us with a fair amount of light. Our skipper called down from the bridge and asked how many troops we had on board, and was told about 200, but as he found that he could not get back to his berth, he decided to go back with what troops he had on board. The midnight news that night gave the names of the paddle steamers which had been sunk and ours was amongst them. I think I can remember the names rightly of those that were sunk - they were the *Royal Sovereign*, *Brighton Belle*, *Brighton Queen*, *Crested Eagle*, *Gracie Fields* and *Waverley*. Both my wife and Mother heard the midnight news and, of course, you can imagine their joy when on the seven o' clock news the error was rectified. I think I can quite understand how that mistake came about. When Commander Buchannan had got his troops on to the other boat he came back to where we had

been berthed and called out for *Medway Queen* and the skipper of the packet which had taken our place probably said we had gone - meaning we had gone back - and Buchannan thought he meant gone down, so he signalled over to that effect. I did hear, but don't know how true it is, that he was killed on the last day of the evacuation.

Albert served on board HMS *Medway Queen* after Dunkirk, minesweeping in the North Sea. He was awarded the Royal Humane Society's certificate for saving a sailor from drowning, and finished the war with a DSM awarded during his time in coastal forces.

Members of HMS Medway Queen's crew - courtesy of MQPS Collection.

John Im Thurn

From his account; supplied by his nephew, James Hamilton-Paterson.

John Im Thurn was an officer cadet (RASC) manning the harbour reception at Ramsgate during operation Dynamo. He and his colleagues had listened to the grumbles about the lack of AA cover and had persistently requested permission to take Bren guns and help. Permission was unintentionally granted by a harassed Brigade Major who was talking to somebody else and said "Yes, yes" to get rid of them. In about five minutes they were aboard various available craft. It was Friday 31st May.

With Jack Feathers and Brian Rayment, John went aboard HMS *Medway Queen*. Soon after they boarded she moved out of the harbour and dropped anchor. About 9am on the Saturday the CO went ashore and after two hours he returned and they sailed. It was only later that John learned that sailings were only on a voluntary basis because of the situation on the other side. They were to convoy the Lymington car ferry, intended to act as a pontoon on Dunkirk beach to help embarkation. She had suffered a serious steering error en-route from the Solent so she was being towed by two Thames tugs, one either side at the bow. The ship towed a string of small boats manned by volunteers from the Medway Towns. They were to ferry troops aboard from the beaches.

About 10 miles off the Fairey Buoy they found a small boat with six occupants rowing to England. They were in civilian clothes and turned out to be Spaniards who had fled from a labour camp near Dunkirk. The CO was suspicious and ordered them to be locked up as a precaution. John was able to interpret for them and they were apparently not pleased when told they were heading for Dunkirk. As they approached La Panne they received orders to proceed to the beach to the east of the mole "by the safest route". John says "This happy phrase meant round or over the minefield which lay between us and the shore. Round it meant a gauntlet run close in down an already enemy-occupied coastline. Over it meant over it - the mines were at 7ft depth - MQ draws 6ft 6ins." The Lymington* car ferry was still in company, under tow by two tugs, and a string of small boats with volunteer crews was towed behind *Medway Queen*. One of the tugs cast her tow and came alongside. John remembers "The tug master was straight out of Punch, bowler hat, broad horizontal red and white striped shirt and an out-grown jacket". He also remembers the conversation:

"How much do you draw?"

"12ft"

"Then you can't come with us. How much fuel have you got?"

"We had 12 hours when we left." (At least 9 hours ago.)

"Have you got a chart?"

"No"

"Will you be all right?"

"Yes."

Medway Queen went on her way with the "kite's tail" of visibly disenchanted volunteers across the minefield. Jack, Brian and I held our collective breaths to lighten ship and loosened our boot laces." They arrived at 11pm. The beach was black with men who waded out to climb aboard. Many had been in action earlier in the day. A sergeant chose his spot, took his water bottle and drained it, he stood for perhaps 15 seconds, then fell flat on his back. It was SRD rum**. He was one of six men carried off when they got back; the other five were dead. Fires beyond the mole were burning, as were houses on the esplanade. By 3am the tide was going out and the ship was nearly full. It was time to leave before she was stranded. The CO was at the door of the port paddle box arguing with a Guards Officer who would not put his wounded aboard without the rest of his company. A strange figure was pushed before him dressed in a pyjama jacket and striped mess overalls. He claimed to be "a lord" but this did not impress the CO and he was secured with the Spaniards.

Medway Queen headed for home. The cadets spent their time controlling the men to ensure an even distribution of weight and between times climbed over the rope barrier to what John describes as the ship's administrative quarters. He says "Damp and exhausted brass hats wondered what scruffy soldiers with white banded shoulder straps were doing. It was simple. They were going to drink whisky!"

*The ferry, MV *Fishbourne*, never did reach the beach and subsequently returned to Ramsgate, towed by the tug *Princess*. See "Isle of Wight Here We Come" by Hugh Compton. Published 1997 by Oakwood Press.
** The SRD rum that knocked out the Sergeant would have come from the supply depot at 135-155 degrees proof (75% alcohol) and was diluted for issue to about 55% alcohol. This is what the Sergeant would have had in his water bottle! The letters 'SRD' stood for either Supply Reserve Depot, or Service Ration Depot.

"Action Stations with the Lewis guns" - courtesy of MQPS Collection.

Norman Penman
From MQ News No. 15 Dunkirk Special Summer 1990.

When it became necessary to evacuate our troops from France I was serving in a battalion based in Chatham. One morning we were asked to volunteer to assist in the evacuation and I ended up on a bus on the way to Dover. We stayed in Dover for about an hour during which time some of the lads persuaded a landlord to open up his pub as they thought it would be a good idea to fill their water bottles with beer. After a while we were taken to Margate where a routine was established whereby an officer would ask for volunteers for a particular job. About a dozen of us who knew each other volunteered together and set off to commandeer some small boats and persuade a ship to take us across to Dunkirk. We were still wearing our webbing kit and carrying rifles so we decided to march to the harbour with all the swank we could muster. This is when the beer proved to be lively and we marched to the sound of corks popping and the discomfort of beer running down our legs. We commandeered our boats and were allowed to hitch them to the stern of *Medway Queen* although we were warned that they would not survive the crossing and as it turned out they did not.

This was the first time I had been out of the UK and it was a great adventure for me. It was dark when we got there and not realising the danger I thought that it was fantastic. Oil tanks were burning, guns firing, and shells exploding. Tracers were floating up and flares like strings of onions were floating down. Although it was spectacular it prevented us from using the harbour and we moved up the coast a little to Bray Dunes. There were troops on the beach but it was dark and we didn't know who they were. The water was shallow here and *Medway Queen* could not get in very close. We were instructed to take the cutter, go ashore and make contact. If we were fired on we were to return! They turned out to be our troops and our part in the evacuation began. We loaded the boat so full that it grounded so a mate and myself jumped into the water to keep it off. From then on it became routine. Row to the beach, fill up, get wet to the neck and take them back to the ship. On some trips we had a motor boat to tow us back and how welcome that was. When we could cram no more men aboard, we returned to offload at Ramsgate. Then it was back to Dunkirk for another session.

Anyone who was at Dunkirk must have memories, and these are mine: the discipline of troops standing chest deep in water waiting to be taken off. The insistence that no hand grenades be taken on board. Being given a packet of five Woodbines each time we got back to the ship and seeing them float away when we jumped into the water back at the beach. Thinking how harmless the shells looked when exploding in the sand until I realised that some of the soldiers who went down were not getting up. Being amazed at how low planes could fly over the sea. Tying a Lewis Gun to the stays so that we could fire back at the planes. Being shown how it could be done by one of the crew members who could hit the planes and was, I believe, decorated for shooting down two planes. The ship keeling over each time an enemy plane approached as everyone took cover on the opposite side.

This was followed by cries of "trim the ship" from the bridge in the hope we could get the paddles back in the water and get some control over the steering. Watching Guardsmen drying their uniforms and polishing their boots so that they could march off at Ramsgate smart enough to have gone on parade.

*HMS **Medway Queen** crew members - courtesy of MQPS Collection.*

Kenneth R Olley

From information supplied by the Olley family.

Kenneth Roy Olley RNVR was a seaman and Quartermaster on board HMS *Medway Queen*. At Dunkirk, in his Captain's words, he "did exceptional service, helping wounded from the beach and keeping the motor launch with a dud engine running, towing troops to ship, for the whole seven trips." Ken said in a newspaper article many years later "it was an experience I shall remember all my life. We pulled the lads out of the water as well as we could. Many of them belonged to the Green Howards regiment". He was recommended for an award by Lt. Cook and this was gazetted on 16th August 1940. He was also awarded a "gratuity" of £20 (equivalent to approximately £1100 in 2020).

Lt. Jolly (Navigator) wrote to Ken in September 1940 expressing his delight at the award of his DSM. "I shall always remember your forceful language when we were in the motor launch together - I think it did more to blister the beaches at Dunkirk than all Jerry's shells". He went on to say that he had settled down as First Lieutenant in HMS *Lorna Doone* (another paddle minesweeper) but that he "missed the tough guys in your seamen's mess and wish I could transfer them all to this ship".

Ken served in *Medway Queen* for some time after Dunkirk, and was married to Vera on the 24th May 1941. They visited *Medway Queen* at least once during her time as a night club on the Isle of Wight.

Photo top Kenneth Olley.
Photo left his DSM medal.
Both courtesy of the Olley family.

William Graham Mathias

By his son, Lt Col David Ashley Mathias DL.
(Vice Lord-Lieutenant for the County of Dyfed)

Born on 23rd October 1920 in Llanelly, South Wales, the son of a foundry moulder. Educated in Bigyn Primary and Stebonheath secondary schools in Llanelly, he began work at the age of 14 as a grocer's assistant. He was known as Graham. At an early age he wished to join the Navy after seeing the battlecruiser *Renown* in Plymouth during a family holiday. His wish became reality when war broke out in 1939, and he immediately took the opportunity to volunteer for the Royal Navy.

It was not until the following May, after the Germans had launched their Blitzkrieg and the Battle for France was being fought (and lost), that he received his 'call up'. He reported to HMS *Ganges* in Shotley, Suffolk, on 16th May 1940 for initial training in the Communications Branch. His arrival there coincided with a deepening crisis, and it is a good indication of just how critical things were, that on or about 27/28th of May, he and a large number of his fellow New Entries, were deployed from Shotley to Kent to assist in the evacuation of the BEF.

Joining *Medway Queen* after less than a fortnight's training, probably at Ramsgate, Ord. Tel. Mathias was to make his first ever sea journey and trip abroad. His recollections of that historic few days were short but very clear and in fact clarify the issue of boats, because he recalled that the ship made her crossings with several extra boats towed astern (a risky seamanship evolution). On arrival in Dunkirk he was employed as boats' crew rescuing men from the water, hauling them into the boat, and out again into the ship. They were in a terrible state of exhaustion and shock. German aircraft constantly harassed both the ships and the men, the dreaded 'Stuka' dive bomber being the most prevalent.

Operation Dynamo closed on 4th June 1940, and Ord. Tel. Mathias returned to HMS *Ganges* to complete his training. In 1990 he was present at Aldershot for the 50th anniversary parade of Dunkirk Veterans and inspected by HM The Queen.

43

Six Lads from Teignmouth

HMS *Medway Queen*'s crew included six lads from Teignmouth, Devon, who joined up in 1939 and were posted to the ship on commissioning. They were Roger Matthews, Jim Day, Bruce Sutton, Bill Keytes, Arthur Maranga and Albert Nason.

Bruce Sutton

From MQ News No. 15 Dunkirk special Summer 1990.

One afternoon in May 1940 the *Medway Queen* left Dover for Dunkirk where our forces were in trouble. A long time before we got there we saw the flames and soon we smelled the fuel oil. No person who was there will forget it. We went six more times, mostly to La Panne but sometimes to Dunkirk Harbour, going around many wrecks.

We had a motor boat which towed another to and from the beach. The army lined up on the shore. I did not see anyone panic or jump the queue. When the ship returned to Ramsgate ladies were waiting with tea and sandwiches and our passengers were whisked away. We fuelled, stored, tidied up and it was time to go again. On one trip we came back in company with *Brighton Belle* and she hit a wreck. We went alongside and they all came aboard before she sank. Fortunately it was a calm day as we were very overloaded. At one time three fighter planes chased each other around near us and one man bailed out but I don't know if he was friend or foe. Once some soldiers with a Bren gun came over to increase our firepower. We had a 12 pounder of Boer War vintage and a Lewis gun but lots of boats had none. Once we were reported sunk

44

on the BBC but next morning they said it was another ship. Among the craft going over was the Massey Shaw (London fireboat), a river vehicle ferry, small merchant coasters and private yachts. The way over was marked by small boats abandoned.

After Dunkirk we had a few days leave and I slept for the first 24 hours. Back aboard the *Medway Queen* we anchored in the Downs in fine weather and caught fish. Later we thought that we were going to end up as the first line of defence and I hoped that we would get a message off before we were sunk. Some said that Dunkirk was a nine days wonder. A destroyer called Sabre did eight trips. We came second with seven.

In a later edition of Medway Queen News Bruce recalled HMS *Medway Queen*'s armament: "We had a 12pdr on the forecastle, a Lewis gun on one sponson and, at one time, we had a Holman Projector on the aft end. For those who do not know it was a tube about four feet long down which a Mills Bomb was to be dropped with the pin out. At the bottom of the tube either steam or a cartridge fired it back up and it exploded a couple of hundred feet in the air. Ours had a cartridge but the steam type, if they were not hot enough, simply rolled the grenade out onto the deck to explode! We also had a reel of wire about waist high on the after deck which was connected to a small barrage balloon. There was also a device on one of the sponsons which sent up a canister containing a small parachute with a wire attached. Once this thing was fired while we were alongside another ship and it landed in her rigging but did no damage."

Jim Day
From MQ News No. 15 Dunkirk Special Summer 1990 and an account by Noreen Chambers in Full Ahead Winter 2012.

In November 1939 Jim, along with several other men from Devon, were to join the naval patrol bases in HMS *Pembroke* in Chatham. They were assigned to HMS *Medway Queen* which had been converted to a minesweeper. The ship's aft saloon had been cut away to allow space for the minesweeping gear. Her name was painted out and replaced with a pennant number. Jim and his friends could not have imagined what lay ahead of them.

In 1990 Jim said "She was my home from November 1939 to 1941 and although I joined other ships later it was *Medway Queen* that sticks in my mind mostly. She made seven journeys, often limping home overcrowded with weary troops, grateful for the hot cocoa she gave them. I was proud to have been a member of the ship's company and over the years have talked about her so much that my daughter had a pen and ink drawing done which now hangs proudly on my lounge wall so that she is constantly in view.

Jim was a member of the MQPS until his death in June 2012. In the summer of 2000 a memorial service on the ship at Damhead Creek was attended by Jim and his wife, May, as well as Bruce and Iris Sutton and Albert and Eileen Nason - all from Teignmouth. This was to mark the 50th anniversary of the Dunkirk evacuation.

Albert T. Nason
As recorded by Len Knight

"When we came close to Dunkirk there was nothing but smoke, thick black smoke from the oil tanks that had been bombed. Medway Queen did not pick up any troops from the harbour itself on that trip but was sent on to the beach at La Panne. We had towed some small motor boats over from England to pick up the troops and on the first morning we got there the boats went off and started loading us up. When we were full we started coming back, there was a girl on the beach dressed as a soldier but they spotted long hair hanging down her back and they wouldn't let her come on board. While we were in Ramsgate getting ready to go over for the seventh trip everyone was saying that it was getting a bit fierce over there. Lt. Cook called the crew together and told everyone to write a postcard to their families and then all hands went ashore to the pub on the jetty where the Captain bought us all a drink. On that last trip while in Dunkirk Harbour we were damaged when a destroyer astern of us was hit. This badly damaged our paddle box and it took us a lot longer to get back than it should have done and we heard on the BBC News that the Medway Queen had been lost. At first we laughed but then we realised that our people at home would have heard the report too. When we got back to Dover we were given six days special leave."

Albert Nason meets Bob Pemberton, one of the men he rescued at Dunkirk - courtesy of Dawlish Gazette.

Roger Matthews
From MQ News No 11, June 1989.

Roger Matthews was also from Teignmouth and served in the Royal Navy for the whole of WWII. For much of that time, including the Dunkirk Evacuation, he served on board HMS Medway Queen. Roger was a keen photographer and many of the photos in our collection were taken by him. Roger was a supporter and member of the MQPS, but sadly passed away in 1989.

K. M. Greig, HMS *Sandown*

We must not forget that the CO *(*Cdr K M Greig DSO Rtd, Actg) and other men from HMS *Sandown* joined *MQ* as additional hands, or replacements for exhausted men, for at least one trip. Unfortunately their names are not known to us.

There must have been other members of the original crew as well. Thomas Russell puts the number of crew at 48 which is rather more men than we have so far identified. Additional crew were allocated for Operation Dynamo, such as William Mathias and Norman Penman, to man the boats bringing troops off the beaches. As William notes, additional boats were taken across and, of course, the Little Ships played their part in ferrying the men out to the larger vessels.

*More members of the wartime crew of HMS **Medway Queen** - courtesy of MQPS collection.*

If any reader is able to identify crew members seen but not named in this and other photos, please do get in touch with the Author or the Medway Queen Preservation Society.

Crew members Jim Day, Roger Matthews and ?? Lewis -
courtesy of MQPS Collection.

Known Names of officers and men rescued from Dunkirk by HMS *Medway Queen*

Name	Picked Up	Unit
Baldwin, Charles James	May 30th/31st	49th (West Riding)
Barton, Frank		RAF Ground crew
Brunt, P. E.		RASC
Callow, John Clayton	May 30th/31st	2nd Lt. 4th Royal Sussex
Chivers, Cyril (Jim)	June 1st/2nd	RASC
Clifford, Oliver		LCpl RASC
Cox, Les	May 29th 30th	Sgt Major
Davis, Alfred		6th Yorks & Lancs
Dervilers, Paul		
Edwards, Albert	May 31st June 1st	
Edwards ,Tom Sydney	May 27th/28th	RASC (driver)
Farnworth, George		Kings Own
Fuller, W.J.C.	May 28th	Royal Navy
Garland, Eric	"Last trip"	6th Yorks & Lancs
George, Alf		Royal Artillery
Gould, G C M	May 30th/31st	2nd Lt. 4th Royal Sussex
Greenwood, Charles		Royal Artillery
Hadfield, Harry		Coldstream Guards
Hankey, Ted		
Harris, Augustus (Gus) Oliver	"Last trip"	WO2, Coy SM RASC
Hill, P C		507 Field Coy RE
Hore	May 30th/31st	Sgt. 4th Royal Sussex
Hopcraft, Reg.		
Howarth ,John		
Knight C. E.		Lieutenant, East Lancashire
Medhurst, Ronald Arthur		LCpl RAMC
Nabarro, Ronald	June 1st/2nd	Cpl. Middlesex Yeomanry
Nix, C F A	May 30th/31st	Major 4th Royal Sussex
Pemberton, Bob		88th Field Rgt. RA
Powell, Albert Henry		Royal Signals
Reid, Claude (Kit)		
Reed, Cyril		RASC
Slade, Harold	May 31st June 1st	RASC (Major)
Skinner, W J	May 31st June 1st	132nd Field Ambulance RAMC
Tozer, V.		Sgt. Royal Military Police
Ward, Leo	June 1st/2nd	Royal Northumberland Fusiliers
Wakinshaw, Les		508 Field Park Coy
Wilson, George B.		RASC

NB "Last Trip" could be either June 2/3 or June 3/4.

DUNKIRK SURVIVORS' MEMORIES OF MEDWAY QUEEN

Alf George
From Full Ahead, Summer 2010

I went to France in 1939 with the 52nd Anti-tank Regiment RA.TA. We moved to Lille in what they called the "phoney war". When the balloon went up we moved into Belgium and then started falling back until we were told we had been cut off by the Germans and that we were moving into France to Arras to break through their lines. We then fell back to La Panne in Belgium where we expected to make a last stand and be killed or captured.

But we moved back again, to the sand dunes near Dunkirk, dropping our gun in a field on the way. We arrived there early morning on, I believe, the 2nd of June. We were told to settle down among the dunes for safety and wait to be called. There weren't many men on the beach so the air attacks had dropped off a bit, just a few on the small groups still on the beaches. In the afternoon we filed down to the mole, passing lots of bodies lying where they had fallen. When we reached the mole, passing bodies on stretchers until we reached where we could look over, I saw a small paddle steamer. I went to pass the Bren gun down to a sailor and he said "drop that in the water". I said "I can't do that" so he said "Oh, give us here".

I climbed over the rail and dropped down on the boat with the help of the sailor. He said to follow on, which I did, and went down below to the cabin where there was a bench seat round the outside where I sat down. It was still daylight and I went to sleep. I was woken by a shell burst. Outside it had become dark but with the flashes from the shells I could see the deck which was covered with stretchers taking every bit of floor space possible. I dropped off again and was next woken up by the anchor being dropped. It was now daylight and one of the soldiers looked out and said "That looks like Margate. I bet they are going to take us back to the other end of France where they are still fighting." But, no, up came the anchor and we moved along the coast to Ramsgate where we moored to a jetty. We had to wait until they had moved the stretchers and then we filed off amid crowds cheering and clapping their hands. We filed up the jetty to some coaches which took us to the railway station, still with crowds lining the route. We then boarded a train and off up north. It seemed as if we had won the war, with the food, drinks and cigarettes that were lavished on us.

Like Eric Woodroffe, Alf became a great supporter of the MQPS. He came forward and helped at events including the 70th anniversary of Dunkirk where he met Eric for the first time. He was guest of honour at other events including the "War and Peace Show" at Paddock Wood where he met up with Vera Lynn, the popular singer from the 1940s who he had previously met when her plane landed at his camp in the desert during a sandstorm.

V Tozer (RMP)
Adapted from his book, *Redcaps in Tin Hats*.

Sgt Tozer and his colleagues were waiting in the sand dunes with no boats in sight. Eventually, on their third day, as the sound of firing drew closer they spotted a ship; HMS **Medway Queen**, a paddle minesweeper. They were so pleased to see her that she was likened to the **Queen Mary**! There were some 15,000 troops on the beach, and the ship stood off by about a mile because of the shallow water. A solitary rowing boat made its way from the ship to the shore.

Earlier that day they had taken charge of some 50 wounded men, thanks to their MP armbands and as the boat approached they saw that it was in the charge of a naval cadet. They shouted "wounded men over here" and the boat headed towards them. They waded out, pulled it in closer and loaded the men in. The water was almost up to the gunwales. Sgt Tozer describes how he stood at the helm like Nelson as they headed out to sea.

By the time they got to the ship water was coming in over the side of the boat and the fit men went over the side to lighten the load, hanging on to the ropes. Everyone else baled with their helmets. The wounded were helped up ropes and onto the deck. There were already about two hundred troops on board. Two more boats came off the beach and then the paddles began turning. Nothing happened, they were stuck on the bottom. The men were so tightly packed that there was no room to rock the ship to free her. Forty soldiers were put off in a boat to lighten the ship and create space and a certain amount of movement became possible. There was a shudder and a movement, the sea turned muddy as the paddles churned. Then the ship broke free and got under way. They picked up the rowing boat while on the move and eventually made it to Ramsgate harbour.

Tom Edwards
Robert J Edwards

This is my granddad's story His name was Tom Sydney Edwards and he was saved at Dunkirk by the **Medway Queen**. During the Second World War (1939, after he was married) he transported food and munitions to the battle front for three years (he was in the Royal Army Service Corps Army Number T/63567). Once he had to drive a truck with no brakes down a steep road with 200 bombs in the back; he followed a convoy so that when he got too fast he could hit the back of the truck in front to slow the lorry down.

In the retreat to Dunkirk, Sydney dumped his lorry over a cliff to prevent the Germans getting the ammunition. He was one of the 338,000 soldiers evacuated from Dunkirk and was on the beach for a day or so before he was evacuated. The first boat he was picked up in was bombed. He was then rescued by another boat

("*Brighton Belle*" I think) which was also sunk, he got some shrapnel in his arm and as he went into the water he grabbed hold of a gramophone (as he could not swim). Eventually he was picked up by another boat, *Medway Queen*, which took him the remainder of the journey. The gramophone was also saved. The wound from the shrapnel meant he was in hospital; his brother William (Bill) was in the same hospital but they did not realize each other was in there until their wives met. He had to have a bone graft (from his leg) and because of this he was discharged from the army as medically unfit and so was kept out of the rest of the war. He was discharged on 18th April 1941.

Cyril (Jim) Chivers
Interviewed in 2013.

Jim was born in Wiltshire in 1918 and joined the Royal Army Service Corps (RASC) in 1933 at the age of 15. Jim's unit went to France as part of the British Expeditionary Force (BEF) attached to the 5th Division.

As the Dunkirk evacuation began Jim's unit was sent inland to pick up troops. In the event this was not possible and orders came to destroy their vehicles and fall back. All but two were destroyed and they began their journey back to Dunkirk. Eventually these two were also destroyed and the men completed their journey on foot. Jim and a friend became separated from the rest of the unit but found them again later.

On arrival Jim waited on the beaches under fire for two days. At first they were at La Panne but soon moved westward towards Dunkirk. Jim's call to embark came on June 1st when he and his colleagues were sent to the East Mole and boarded *Medway Queen* under shell fire. He thinks this was late in the afternoon or evening but remembers little except some surprise that the crew were Royal Navy and not civilian. They were sent below deck and fell asleep almost immediately. The night of June 1st/2nd was one of the last pickups for British personnel and the signal concluding the British evacuation was sent the following evening.

Jim awoke early the next morning in Ramsgate when the ship berthed. They were marched to the station and put on a train which took them to Rugeley (Birmingham). They spent two days there and Jim remembers that soldiers based there full time were confined to barracks while the Dunkirk survivors were allowed to visit the town. They were then sent to Insch in Aberdeenshire where they were all given two days leave. It apparently took most of that time just to get home!

Charles James Baldwin
Melanie Baldwin

Melanie's late husband's father, Charles James Baldwin, was evacuated from Dunkirk by HMS *Medway Queen*. Charles had been in the battle for Caestre from where they fell back to Dunkirk. He survived Dunkirk with no injuries - at least not physical ones. He left an account and says "they boarded after 7am as the bridge they needed to cross was on fire at one end". Once aboard, they were offered "tea, bread, butter and bully". Then "We disembarked at Ramsgate at 12noon and left for Shrewsbury for a few days' rest". *Medway Queen*'s log for Dunkirk shows an 11.55am arrival at Ramsgate on May 31st.

From other timings recorded it was about a 4 hour trip although the route varied according to circumstances. That fits Charles' account and it's safe to deduce that he was brought home on this trip. After Dunkirk Charles served with the 49th (West Riding) Regt. Reconnaissance Corps but, sadly was mortally wounded and died at the age of 25 on the 5th September 1944. He is buried in Le Havre.

Charles' brother, Martin, was too young to serve in the war but was obviously deeply affected by the loss of Charles. He trained as a fitter and one of his home projects was a working model of a paddle steamer engine, representative of that on *Medway Queen* (photo, by Melanie Baldwin) in tribute to Charles.

Martin passed away in January 2019 and Melanie has generously made the model available on loan to the Medway Queen Visitor Centre.

John Clayton Callow (2nd Lt. 4th Royal Sussex Regiment)
Extracted from Chris Smith's *Roads to Dunkirk.*

".... I found a military policeman, who told me to my great surprise, that this was Bray Dunes. I had arrived at the beach without knowing it. After a lot of chasing about I found that the beach had been split up into areas; and at long last found ours. People were very surprised to see us, as they had been told that our Division had been cut off and had surrendered!

About an hour after we got to the beaches a few other men from the Regiment arrived, so we tried to join one of the many queues waiting for boats. Nothing happened by midnight, so we went back into the sand-dunes, and went to sleep. Six of us slept between two dry blankets with a groundsheet and six wet blankets on top of us to keep the wind out, and didn't wake until ten the next morning, Thursday. Thursday is very confused. More of the battalion arrived, including the Colonel, and we all tried in turn to get tickets allowing us to embark. The Colonel and about a hundred men got on a destroyer after tea, leaving Major Nix, Captain Gould and I with a hundred and fifty men still on the beach. No more boats came in owing to the tide, so we scraped around for some food; we had eaten nothing since eight o'clock the previous evening. I found some tins of French bully beef, enough for one per man in my platoon; that was unbelievably tough but most welcome.

Water was very scarce, and I refused to allow any of my men to drink alcohol. What little water we did get was very salty.

The Germans then put about a dozen shells down on our sector of the beach, but our men were grand, just lying flat where they were. Some units who had no officers left, or whose officers had embarked, started running, but the panic fortunately was quickly stopped. At long last boats appeared, and they came all through the night, taking off our men gradually. Five or six trips were made with two boats, as they took only about fifteen men each, and each round trip took about an hour. At about five, there were only a dozen or so left, all my platoon, they refused to go on board until I went. At last I was pulled into the boat, feeling very numb as I had been standing in the water up to my waist for a couple of hours, and that was the last boatload of the 4th Battalion to be taken off, and the last for that ship.

She was a paddle-steamer, the '*Medway Queen*', which I suppose normally took two hundred people from Westminster to Southend in peacetime. This time though she had about a thousand on board. What heroes those sailors, Royal Navy, were. They had been doing this for five days, without an hour's sleep, and yet every man within an hour had had a hot cup of tea, our first for four days, and a bully beef sandwich, the first bread the men had eaten for over a week. The officers, about twenty, were accommodated in the mess, and were treated royally. All our clothes were sent down to the boiler room to dry, and then we slept, on the floor, on the tables, in chairs, anywhere. When we reached Ramsgate at eleven on the Friday morning, we had left France at five, the skipper told us that they had shot down two dive-bombers on the trip. None of us had heard anything!"

Roads to Dunkirk has been published by Chris J. Smith and is available on Amazon, as an e-book or as a paper-back. It starts with the personal account of John Callow, a lieutenant in the 4th Royal Sussex in the spring of 1940, written in 1941.

P.C. Hill
From Medway Queen News No 15 Dunkirk Special 1990.

I waded out from Bray Dunes to be picked up by the *Medway Queen* with 80 other lads of the 507 Field Company RE., plus some 400 others from various units on the morning of 29th or 30th May* - a bit hazy on the actual day. Once on board, greeted by Captain Cook with a bar of Bourneville chocolate, relieved of our spare ammunition for their machine guns and then below decks to the galley for a much needed sweet tea and a huge corned beef sandwich. After a couple of shells came over, a bit too close for comfort, we moved off from the beach before the morning mist had cleared to land at Margate.

*Margate as a destination suggests a date of May 30th.

George Barclay Wilson
From The Medway Queen, first published 2013.

George Barclay Wilson joined the Royal Army Service Corps and in 1940 found himself in France driving a lorry towards Dunkirk. On arrival he was told to ruin the engine and head for the beach where he joined thousands of others waiting to be picked up. He boarded the *Crested Eagle* from the East Mole just as a bomb hit the ship but was lucky enough to get back on the Mole. He then boarded *Medway Queen* and was taken back to Britain. George's father was Mr. Thomas Hunter Rickson Wilson who was the engineer responsible for *Medway Queen*'s delivery voyage from Scotland in 1924. He was so taken with Rochester that he decided to relocate there with his family.

Major Harold C. G. Slade OBE
Tim and Andrew Claringbull

Stories from *Medway Queen*'s history in peace and war keep coming to our attention and we do all we can to record them as part of our ship's history. One such is Harold Slade who was rescued by HMS *Medway Queen* at Dunkirk. Major Harold Slade went to France to join the British Expeditionary Force in January 1940. He was in the Royal Army Service Corps, attached to the 44th Division, and responsible for supplying provisions to the troops. His principal role was ensuring the petrol supply across Northern Europe and he was in charge of some 14,000 men. In May, as the BEF fell back towards the coast, it became increasingly difficult to find and transport the stores required and they had to rely on a mix of local purchases and requisitions where purchase was not possible. Major Slade kept a diary of which his family have kindly provided excerpts recording his experiences following the German invasion on May 10th. He tells of falling back under fire, of roads clogged with refugees and of expeditions to find food for the troops.

On May 28th he moved off in the direction of Dunkirk. He visited advanced divisional HQ with supplies early in the morning, assisted some refugees and motored to Bray Dunes. On the 29th he arrived on Dunkirk beach at 6.00am. There were tens of thousands of troops there. He arranged, late in evening, for all troops to embark but found that they had been sent in the direction of Dunkirk. The next day he saw troops off during the day, hampered by a shortage of small boats. Little food was available. "Jerry shelled beach at 5pm. No damage done by bombers. Spent night wading through water looking for boats."

On the 31st May they found a boat at 3.00am and boarded the *Medway Queen* with officers of Signals and other regiments. They were landed in Ramsgate and moved on to Shrewsbury by train. "Great reception en route. With KSLI (King's Shropshire Light Infantry)." He made sure that all of his troops had safely left Dunkirk beach before he embarked. The welfare of his troops was always his priority.

On the 1st June he walked into Shrewsbury to the cinema where he saw "If I Had A Million".

Major Slade was later promoted to Colonel and awarded the OBE. Relatives of Harold Slade visited *Medway Queen* recently and we are very grateful to Tim and Andrew Claringbull for allowing us to use their grandpa's story and the photographs. All images are their copyright.

> FRI.—(Battle of Jutland, 1916—Boer War ended, 1902—Union
> 31 Day, South Africa, 1910.)
> *formed boat at 3 am + brought*
> *the Medway Queen. with officers*
> *of Signals, Sussex + Rufk Regt*
> *man from Ramsgate to Shrewsbury*
> *Great reception en route.*
> *with KSLI.*

Oliver Clifford
Kathy Ventham

My Dad, Oliver Clifford, was a Lance Corporal in the RASC and was rescued from Dunkirk by HMS *Medway Queen*, although we do not have the date he was picked up. When Dad was marching on the retreat to Dunkirk he was in a great deal of pain with his feet. It took a medic in England to tell him he had been marching with his boots on the wrong feet!

After Dunkirk he went on to serve in Bombay and the Middle East. He was with the Desert Rats, driving ammunition lorries. He served at El Alamein and was also at Normandy for the D Day landings. He was very good friends with the family Gondre who owned and ran the Pegasus Bridge cafe.

Frank Barton
From Full Ahead, Winter 2008

The Medway Queen Preservation Society's "Reading Support Group" had a publicity and fund-raising stall on behalf of *Medway Queen* at a canalside event in Newbury, Berkshire. I was looking out over the field, wondering when (or even if) the next customer was coming along when I noticed one of the British Legion gentlemen walking across the field. He spotted us, stopped in his tracks, and then made a beeline towards our stall. It was Frank Barton who until that day had not realised the *Medway Queen* was still around. Suddenly the day was a success - for both of us! Frank was a LAC (RAF ground crew) in France in 1939/40. He told his story to Kathie Clark for our Full Ahead magazine in 2008:

"My journey to the *Medway Queen* began in September 1939. A midnight dash on a RN destroyer from Southampton to Cherbourg - ground crews of 4 and 13 squadrons. We made our way to an old WWI grass airfield at Monchy-Lagache near Perone. Here in old farm buildings we spent the winter doing photographic work of the Siegfried Line. The Germans let us because when the push came on 10th May 1940 it was from Belgium and the Ardennes that they came, with such force and strength that we were dazed. In weeks we lost all our Lysander aircraft, brave crews shot out of the sky by 109s and the rest shot up on the ground.

So, with no planes we were not much use. After all we were ground crew - mechanics, riggers, armourers, etc., so we were ordered to filter in with the army who by now were making a fighting retreat to the only port left open to us - Dunkirk. Having got there we spent two nights in a park, living in slit trenches, awaiting orders. We had no kit, having to burn everything in the retreat. We had our rifles and ammo, which we were told to keep, and nothing else. Food? We raided the overturned lorries loaded with food-stuff that had been destined to go up to the front. Overhead I won't mention. History has recorded that for all time. The Germans did their very best to see that we did not evacuate.

Then the order came through to proceed in single file to the docks, using what cover we could. We arrived alongside the Mole and there was a welcome sight - the *Medway Queen* berthed alongside the Mole. We were the lucky ones. One humorous situation I will mention - an army despatch rider had his motor bike with him and was demanding it be taken on board. The sailor on the gang-plank said "Give it to me, I'll see to it". He sent the soldier on his way, wheeled the bike down the jetty and tipped it into the sea! The orders were men and their rifles and I think it was only walking wounded; no stretcher cases. Then we stuck on a sandbank and went round and round and then away. We were all very tired and hungry as we had been on the run for two weeks - we were exhausted. I found a corner under the bridge I thought it might protect me from the gunfire as bombs were dropping all the time. I slept all the way home. With hindsight a silly thing to do, but see what trust we had in the crew, and we were so tired. The next step was Dover - dark, and blue lights - and being led to a train and being taken to Tidworth Army Camp. Now food and a bath and a train again to Ringway RAF station near Manchester Airport. We were kitted out with all new gear and sent home for some leave."

Frank's subsequent war service included North Africa, Sardinia and Italy. He returned to the UK on June 26th 1945. He described this as paying "my debt to the *Medway Queen* and her brave crew for rescuing me all those years ago and so put one small cog back into the war machine to eventually bring victory." After discovering the ship was still in existence Frank became a great supporter of the Medway Queen Preservation Society and did his bit to help promote the cause. He was made an honorary life member of the society in 2008. Sadly, Frank passed away in Newbury on 20th January 2012.

P. E. Brunt
Major P. E. Brunt MBE ERD

I mobilised with the 3rd Infantry Division in August 1939 and was posted to the 3rd Division RASC. Our Divisional Commander was Major General B. L. Montgomery. We crossed over to France in September 1939 and spent the winter and early spring training in Northern France. On May 10th 1940, when the Germans invaded France, Belgium and Holland we moved forward into Belgium to the line of the River Dyle, which included the town of Louvain where we met the Germans. After several days of fighting we held our positions but then had to fall back to conform with the French, who were in full retreat on our right flank. As the situation worsened we were told to immobilise our vehicles, then make our way to the coast which was about 10 miles away.

We arrived at the seaside resorts of La Panne and Furnes in the early hours of May 26th. There were many thousands of troops on the beaches but no embarkation taking place and little or no organisation. I remember seeing four destroyers coming towards the beach at great speed, then turning sharply and disappearing over the horizon. We nevertheless managed to despatch most of our troops during the next three days.

The attacks by German aircraft were numerous but did not cause many casualties among the troops on the beach for two reasons. First the sand was very soft, consequentially the bombs and shells penetrated quite deeply before exploding. Secondly, the oil tanks in Dunkirk Harbour were ablaze and the dense black smoke formed an umbrella over the embarkation beaches. During our time on the beach the paddle steamer *Devonia* was bombed in Dunkirk harbour; she made her way out of the port and came at great speed towards the beach where we were. She was burning amidships and men were being forced up into the bows by the flames. She ran aground and then the troops had to jump into the sea. Those who could not swim were drowned.

By the evening of May 29th we had managed to evacuate all our personnel, with the exception of myself and five others, and as the beach was being heavily shelled we had to take cover in the sand dunes. On the morning of June 1st, at about 3am, we walked into the water. It was a very quiet morning with no gunfire or bombing and only just beginning to get light. Suddenly I heard a voice calling "Soldier, soldier". I called to the others and we waded deeper into the water. Then we saw a ship's lifeboat with two sailors holding it in position with their oars. We waded to the boat and I remember clinging to the side. One of the sailors grabbed me by the seat of my pants and tumbled me into the boat! I asked him if they were going to row us out to a larger boat; he replied that a motor launch would come for us and sure enough in a few minutes a launch appeared and took us in tow. We soon came alongside a paddle steamer and how well I remember seeing the name above the paddle box, *Medway Queen*. Climbing aboard was like boarding the *Queen Mary*. The first person I saw was, I presumed, the skipper. He was not in uniform but in a grey pullover and no cap. He asked me if there were any more troops on the beach.

I said there were none where we had come from, and if I were him I'd set sail as soon as possible for as soon as it became light we would be bombed. He told me he could not sail yet as he had only two hundred troops on board.

He then told me to go below where I'd be given something to eat and drink. When I went to what I think was the wardroom I was handed a mug of tea and the largest ham sandwich I had ever seen, or ever since seen! It must have been six inches square by three inches thick! Unfortunately I could not do justice to it as we'd been four days without food and with only a little muddy water to drink, which we'd managed to scrape from the bottom of a well belonging to a sanatorium near the beach. However, the tea went down very well and did wonders for my throat which seemed to have closed up.

The wardroom was rather crowded but I found an unoccupied corner where I sat on the floor with my back against the wall. We did not sail until 6am, by which time we had picked up a full load of troops. After being under way for about half an hour there was the sound of the engine room bell ringing and the engine stopped, followed by a loud bang right above my head. My thoughts were that we'd been hit and would now sink. Suddenly the serving hatch was pulled back and our cheery steward called out "It's all right chaps, we got that aircraft up the backside!" It seemed they had fired at a German aircraft from a gun on the stern. Whether they did hit it or not I never knew.

The rest of the voyage was without incident and we duly arrived at Ramsgate where we were put on a train, eventually arriving at Southport in Lancashire. In retrospect I wish I had thanked the skipper for my rescue but can only put down my lack of good manners to the fact that after four days and nights on the beach, with only a very small amount of muddy water, our morale was not very high.

Les Cox
Medway Queen News, Summer 2000

Sergeant Major Les Cox has left us a harrowing account of the retreat to Dunkirk and the evacuation from the beaches. This is his story from their approach to the beach.

The journey continued towards Dunkirk, although we did not know where we were going. Then we ran out of petrol and had to start marching on foot across open country, constantly harassed by the Stuka dive bombers. We finally came to a road with tram lines and we halted in a large shrubbery where we were unable to get any food at all - it had now been seven days - it was about 10pm and we started off again, still not knowing where we were headed. After about 10 minutes we were halted and returned to the shrubbery where we were reorganised and left behind everything hanging on us that made a noise or clinked. Leaving us with rifle, bayonet, 50

59

rounds of .303 ammunition and a side pack which held personal things like razor, soap, towel, etc. We then started off again, this time in single file column each side of the road with strict orders: no smoking, not to talk, take advantage of every front garden, shop doorway and keep in touch with the man in front. We finally crossed the promenade on to the beach and fell down to rest.

When dawn broke I had another shock. The beach was, as far as you could see, covered in khaki figures, some dead, some wounded and screaming for their mothers, or God, to help them - it was awful. Some bodies at the water's edge were rolling in and out as the waves moved them. The noise was indescribable with warships at sea firing shells into the hinterland over our heads with a continual scream. The German fighters were strafing the beaches up and down with engines roaring. The Dunkirk installations were on fire and belching black smoke, they said the smoke clouds were a mile high. A strange Sergeant Major formed us up into units of about 30, 15 standing and 15 kneeling, to fire at the German fighters as they came over (I don't think we hit anything although I did see one come down in the sea).

Later on our party was formed into columns of threes and marched into the sea to await the navy boats which were called whalers and were like very large row boats with four sailors rowing each one. At this time Naval Petty Officers were walking along the water's edge shouting for anyone who could handle a small boat on a falling tide. Large lorries were being driven into the sea until their engines stopped, then another drove up behind and pushed them out a bit further and so on and soldiers were clambering through the lorries over the cabs and on to the next one. Our lot were standing in the sea and gradually moving forward as another whaler came in and took another load out to sea. In my case, being small and short, the water was soon up to my chest (we were still dressed in army uniform, boots, gaiters and overcoats). The army says it is inclement weather until the 1st June when overcoats were to be discarded. It was the 29th May! We finally got onto the *Medway Queen*, paddle steamer, where we were stripped of our rifles and ammunition. The ship was really packed and I began to feel the lack of food - it had been 8 days now. Two paddle steamers moved off together and we had been under way for 10 minutes when the other paddler* took a direct hit and we stopped to pick up survivors. This made it more difficult on board; we were really dangerously overcrowded and it was impossible to move. The two sets of wide promenade stairs at each end of the ship were cleared and two NCOs were posted with orders to shoot any soldiers from below who tried to rush the decks. The only ones allowed on deck were the Bren gunners. A Naval officer through his megaphone said they knew the channel had been mined by the Germans during the night before, so we were going to sail up the channel hugging the French coast as far as the North Foreland, where we were to cross to the English side and sail back along the English coast until we reached Ramsgate, this took eight hours!

It was quite noisy when we arrived at Ramsgate. The police had fixed telegraph poles across the roads to the quay, holding back hundreds of people, some of whom were shouting out the names of their loved ones. Others had improvised placards by name or regiment printed on them. We were taken to the railway station and we got on a train that was waiting there - 6 men to a compartment. By this time I was so tired and hungry I really did not care what happened. The people whose gardens backed on to the railway had broken down their garden fences, climbed up the embankment and gave us tea, sandwiches, cigarettes, chocolates etc. Food at last. Oh Boy! The trains leaving Ramsgate at that time were nose to tail, moving at about 1 mile per hour, anything to get the troops away. I told the boys in the carriage that I was a Londoner and would be home in an hour and promptly fell asleep. When I awoke I knew we were not going to London but were going in the opposite direction. We finished up about 10pm at Devizes in Wiltshire where we were not well received. Apparently Devizes in peacetime was the depot for the Pay Corps. They were turned out of their "spiders" (elongated Nissan huts) and put in tents in the surrounding fields while we occupied their spiders.

*In another reference to Les, the Spring 2003 edition of Full Ahead suggested this could have been HMS *Brighton Belle* but she was lost the previous day and off the English coast, not French. A more likely candidate is HMS *Waverley*, one of 6 paddle minesweepers lost in Operation Dynamo, which was sunk on 29th May 1940.

George Farnworth
From "Full Ahead", Autumn 2012 Brian Goodhew

George Farnworth was in the 5th King's Own Regiment in position around Lille in France. All was quiet at first but after a while it all started to happen. The German army broke through the Ardennes and for George it was a succession of long marches, blowing up bridges and taking up positions alongside canals and hill tops. George says they "were being blasted with heavy shell fire wherever they tried to hold". George remembered marching night and day with no sleep and covering up to 30 miles. Sleep was just forgotten.

By June 1st they reached the perimeter area just outside La Panne. It was here that what was left of the various units formed a defence line to protect the troops waiting on the beaches to be picked up. After heavy fighting it was George and the King's Own's time to proceed to Dunkirk beach to wait their turn. George said "we arrived at the beach which was in dreadful chaos". They saw "some Coldstream Guards arrive, and they marched onto the beach as if they were on a parade ground. Sadly a shell came over and landed in their midst. There was not a lot left of those fine soldiers."

After many hours of shelling at about midnight, the Sergeant Major came over and gave orders to the men to wade out into the water until it came up to their chests. George was still carrying his rifle and a Bren gun but luckily was soon hauled onto a rowing boat and the overloaded boat made it out to the larger ship which in this case was the *Medway Queen*.

George, like many of the troops, was exhausted, found a space and promptly fell asleep, only to wake up the next morning, Sunday 2nd June, to be greeted with piles of sandwiches. "Wonderful!" said George.

William John Cottam Fuller (HMS *Brighton Belle*)
From notes supplied by his grandson, Tim
West.

William Fuller was a Lieutenant on HMS
Brighton Belle, another ship of the 10th
minesweeping flotilla, commanded by Lt. L.
K. Perrin RNVR. Returning from their first
trip to Dunkirk on the morning of 28th May
HMS *Brighton Belle* struck a submerged
wreck off the Kent coast and began to sink.
HMS *Sandown* and HMS *Medway Queen*
stood by to rescue the men and Lieutenant
Fuller was one of those saved by *Medway*

*HMS **Brighton Belle** sinking, taken from the bridge of HMS **Medway Queen** by signalman Eric Woodroffe.*

Queen. Tom Edwards also told of being rescued from HMS *Brighton Belle* by
Medway Queen and her crew (page 51).

According to his daughter, Mary Marsh, Lt. Fuller had a few days to replace lost
kit and uniform after the sinking and was then posted to HMS *Glen Usk* in the 8th
Minesweeping Flotilla based in North Shields. By July 1941 he is listed as in
command of *Glen Usk* and in 1943 he travelled to Seattle, USA, to take command
of a brand new minesweeper, HMS *Pique*. In due course he was promoted to
Lieutenant Commander and he was awarded the DSC in the New Year's Honours
list of January 1945.

Medway Queen Sunk!
Tim West also passed on copies of the previously elusive (and false) press reports
of *Medway Queen*'s sinking. Six paddle minesweepers were lost in the operation:
Brighton Belle (28th May), *Gracie Fields* (28th May), *Waverley* (29th May),
Crested Eagle (29th May), *Devonia* (31st May) and *Brighton Queen* (1st June).
HMS *Medway Queen* survived but was reported missing by press and radio. The
press cuttings of this that we have are undated but Albert Skinner relates an (also
undated) incident while loading at the Mole that probably gave rise to the reports.
Jack Skinner's diary gives a specific date of June 4th for the crew learning of the
reports and sending telegrams of reassurance to their families. Putting the two
together it would appear that the incident took place on the night of 2nd/3rd of
June, when she did load at the Mole, and the reports went out late in the evening of
the 3rd and in the morning papers of 4th June.

Leslie Wakinshaw
From Full Ahead, Summer 2008

Leslie went to France with the 508 Field Park Company in the early months of the
Second World War. He recalled that "We were sent to Paris and it was like a
holiday camp. Then everything kicked-off. We thought that as soon as hostilities

broke out, we'd just walk through the Germans. We were reading in the papers that the Germans didn't have this and didn't have that and even had wooden tanks. When we saw them in battle we couldn't believe it.

The regiment was split up as we were needed all over as engineers. We were making for Dunkirk when a dispatch rider said we had to go and blow a bridge and the Ordnance Corps would deliver the explosives. Corporal Morgan took four men and they waited for nearly eight hours, but the explosives never arrived. But this also meant we were separated from the main convoys. Leslie and his Geordie mates hid in a village while part of a German armoured division passed through. Then, later that same night, some Frenchmen came and said that German sympathisers had taken over a building and were sending information to the enemy. Jack Cole, our quarter master sergeant, took four lads and came back with six of the sympathisers. The French wanted us to shoot them, but we couldn't do that. We handed them to the police. We got to within 10 miles of Dunkirk when we were told the beach had been bombed to bits and we would have to go to Gravelines, six miles south.

They told us to make our wagons useless. There were a lot of French around, but their vehicles didn't have petrol. Jack wanted to let them syphon ours, but an MP went around puncturing the tanks and letting the petrol spill out. When we reached the beach it was in chaos and nobody seemed to know what was going on. Eventually a young naval officer arrived. He called all the army officers together and Jack, being our highest rank, went with them. When he came back he said that the young lad had organised more in two hours than the rest of the army officers had all day. There were men swimming out to boats and men being rowed to bigger craft, but we were directed to the *Medway Queen*.

We were lucky and managed to wade to it. It was packed but 14 of us Geordies got on it. They crammed us on the boat and took us back to Blighty. When we got back they couldn't get us off quick enough because they wanted to go back to save more. We must have done well in France because Jack got the Military Medal and Alfie Baldwin of Gateshead got the Distinguished Conduct Medal, which was unheard of in such a small unit."

Les became an honorary life member of the Medway Queen Preservation Society in 2008 and did a considerable amount of fundraising for us until his death in August 2011.

Charles Greenwood
Information from the Daily Telegraph obituary, September 2008.

Charles Greenwood was a gunnery officer in the Royal Artillery and was another man rescued by *Medway Queen* although we have no further details. His obituary mentions that in the retreat to Dunkirk he needed to break into a safe to obtain the battery's funds enlisting the skills of one of his men whose peacetime profession had been "rather dubious" to achieve that.

Ronald Medhurst
Dick Medhurst

My dad was Ronald Arthur Medhurst, born on 5th July 1917. I believe he was a Lance Corporal in the Royal Army Medical Corps and was rescued from Dunkirk by HMS *Medway Queen*. This photo was taken whilst he and his wife, Win, were on honeymoon and probably on the same day as their trip on the *Medway Queen*. I don't know more as he didn't talk about it. Sadly he died in 1982.

Leo Ward
Nick Coggins

Medway Queen arrived at Margate at 6.30am on 2nd June 1940*. On board was my great uncle, Leo Ward, a former miner from Tudhoe Colliery, Durham. He was a pre-war regular recalled to the colours for WWII. He survived Dunkirk with the 4th battalion, Royal Northumberland Fusiliers, but was killed two years later in Libya. He is one of the thousands of British troops who fought for their families, their mates and homes, and who died not knowing if their nation would be saved or enslaved.

*Brigadier CN Bradley's History of the Royal Northumberland Fusiliers in WW2, taken from battalion diaries, states that the battalion was picked up from the East Mole by *Medway Queen*. He gives the date as 1st June but this does not tally with the Captain's report and it may have been the following night. Confusion between Margate and Ramsgate is also fairly common.

Albert Edwards
From Full Ahead, Summer 2009

I was called up in June 1939 and went to Aldershot to train. I was then sent to France in November where I went to a camp in a place called Pornichet, a seaside town, to get sorted out. Then I was sent to Northern France to start defence work on the French/Belgian border.

Then on 10th May we had orders to kit up and move into Belgium where we destroyed about three bridges and blocked the roads. On our way back we were stopped by Red Cap Police and ordered to put our vehicles in a field to be destroyed. The German planes were attacking the French convoys including women and children. We stopped at a house to try to get a drink but there was no one there and no water, so we decided to drink some red wine. I took a drink but it was awful as it was red wine vinegar.

We got to the beach on Saturday 31st May, my 21st birthday. It was crowded and I still could not get a drink. Twice I went into the sea to try and get on a boat for England. In the end I was taken off from the Mole Pier by the *Medway Queen*. We landed in Dover on 1st June 1940.

Eric Garland
Information from The Times obituary, 29th January 2016.

In 1940 Eric Garland was in the 6th York and Lancaster Regiment. He won the MC for "conspicuous bravery" while carrying out a motorcycle reconnaissance, looking for a route for his unit near Wormhoudt. He showed bravery again the following day rescuing wounded men from a bombed ammunition store. Not long afterwards Eric found himself on board HMS *Medway Queen* with around a thousand other soldiers. *Medway Queen* is described as an estuary paddle steamer transformed into a minesweeper and as "one of the stars of the evacuation" which has claimed three enemy aircraft shot down. This was on *Medway Queen*'s seventh and last trip when one paddle sponson was damaged while loading at East Mole. Eric was asleep on deck when they finally docked in Ramsgate.

Augustus (Gus) Harris
Philip Harris

My father, Augustus (Gus) Oliver Harris, was a WO2 or Company Sergeant Major with the RASC (Royal Army Service Corps). He told me he was evacuated from Dunkirk and that he was taken off on a Thames paddle steamer and thought the name was "*The Medway*". I can only think it was the *Medway Queen* as he also used to mention an army officer he met on the return who I have worked out after reading the obituary may have been Eric Garland MC as my Father described him as a bit of a hero to the others on board at the time. I have put this together from the memories of my father who died in 2006. He went right through the war, serving in North Africa in the 8th Army to VE day.

Reg Hopcraft
From Full Ahead, Autumn 2013

Reg was on the beach at Bray Dunes when a group of Royal Engineers came marching towards him. They halted and a corporal divided them into two groups. One group started digging a trench and the others took their clothes off and swam out to sea. When they returned they were in a large rowing boat (six oars). Men got on board and were rowed out into the channel. The boat returned and Reg was invited to board but he allowed others to go ahead of him as he had watched the previous loading.

At the earlier loading men went into the water on either side of the boat, then were helped into it, one from each side to maintain an even keel. Reg noticed that the first to go out were up to their necks in water so when the right number had gone forward he took his place and was assisted aboard. He only got his ankles wet. With the Engineers at the oars they rowed out to the Kent paddle steamer, *Medway Queen*, where Reg was taken down near the boilers. He was able to remove his wet clothes and hang them to dry.

There he was with hope in his heart and probably a smile on his face thinking of his good fortune when a small hatch opened and a great wave of water came in and soaked him. It was fortunate that he was near the boiler and by the time they got back to Blighty he was dry again and dressed. As they disembarked a soldier by his side remarked "that was a close one". "What was?" asked Reg, and the soldier said "the bomb that just missed us!"

William John Skinner
Jane Logan

My father, William John Skinner, served in 132 Field Ambulance, RAMC. He married his fiancée, Ruby May, on 9th September 1939 whilst on his two day leave before being called up for service. He was with the BEF in France during the retreat to Dunkirk.

The battalion diary tells us that they fell back to Nouveaumonde on 25th May through roads clogged with heavy traffic. They experienced some difficulty in getting rations and were forced to supplement the food issued with eggs, chickens and even a pig found locally. On 27th May they were ordered to make straight for Dunkirk, harried by air attacks and enemy tanks. They arrived on the beach at Bray Dunes on 28th having had to cross a damaged canal bridge on foot over a single plank. They reported for embarkation and were told to "go away and write a nominal role". When they returned "the Embarkation Office had closed". After being shelled and bombed they got away in small parties over the next few days. The main group embarked from the Mole in unrecorded vessels at 9.45pm on 30th May, reassembling at Castle Bromwich some three weeks later.

John Skinner was picked up on 1st of June by HMS *Medway Queen* from the beach at Malo-les-Bains just to the east of Dunkirk harbour. The ship's log states that they arrived at Malo at about 4pm where they suffered an air attack but shot down one of the aircraft. They left France at 2.45am on 2nd of June and landed at Ramsgate later that morning.

Bob Knight
Robin Knight

Bob Knight was a Motor Contact Liason Officer with the 1st Battalion, East Lancashire Regiment, part of 42 Division in France. He was one of the few officers evacuated twice from France in 1940 (Dunkirk and then St. Nazaire in Operation

Ariel). He was on the dockside when HMT *Lancastria* was sunk with the loss of thousands of lives.

The battalion arrived at Dunkirk around the 2nd of June and Bob's company were directed to a beach near the village of Ghyvelde, near Bray Dunes. The sea was miles out and they had to wade out to small boats for transfer to larger ships lying off shore. Bob recalled that "we were little interfered with by the enemy during the evacuation". He returned to Ramsgate on HMS *Medway Queen* where the men were sent to the railway station and put on the next available train. There were about a dozen East Lancashire men on the train and after a "hellish 24 hour journey" they found themselves at a reception camp outside Durham. Bob recorded that on the journey they received "food, tea, etc. provided by kindly ladies at any station where we stopped". From the Durham camp the men gradually returned to their proper units and Bob rejoined his battalion at Northallerton in Yorkshire.

Cyril Reed
From Full Ahead, Autumn 2004

Cyril Reed was a driver with the RASC at the time of Dunkirk. He visited *Medway Queen* in August 2004 with his family and it was the first time he had seen the ship since he was picked up from the beaches of Dunkirk in 1940. He was a non-swimmer and was pulled out to the ship by ropes along with a comrade in a state of collapse after wading out to her. Once on board he rested alongside the engine room where, after a bite to eat and drink, he slept until arriving home, having no recollection of the journey.

Ronald Nabarro
From his own account

Ron joined the TA in 1938 (Middlesex Yeomanry signals regiment) and was mobilised on 28th August 1939. He was initially stationed at the Duke of York's and later with the War Office as a radio operator. He changed his age to 19 in order to stay with the unit when it went to France in November 1939. In the retreat to Dunkirk Ron was detailed to stay behind and destroy their vehicles and equipment. He was assigned a despatch rider and bike because they were several miles from the coast. They arrived at La Panne beach in due course where they agreed to separate. Ron made for the Mole at Dunkirk and after boarding *Medway Queen* at night fell asleep until a few miles from home arriving on 2nd June. Ron's unit was part of the 5th British Infantry Division who became known as The Globetrotters because they travelled to more overseas destinations than any other unit.

Ron visited *Medway Queen* in Ramsgate in 2015 and we think he is our last remaining Dunkirk Survivor. 99 years young!

Jack Skinner (left) with two crewmates on HMS Medway Queen - courtesy of MQPS collection.

French binoculars given to Jack by an evacuated French Officer - courtesy of Geoff Skinner.

JACK SKINNER'S DIARY
("VERY NEARLY HEROES")

Able Seaman Jack Skinner kept a diary during the early part of 1940. A practice not encouraged by the authorities although it contains little detail. It agrees very closely with the more official accounts of HMS *Medway Queen*'s adventures at Dunkirk.

Sunday 26th May 1940 Plenty of action round here last night. Jerry had a hot reception from shore we didn't get a pot at any. A quiet day, one alarm this morning.

Monday 27th May 1940 Recalled to Dover for provisions and after a lot of mystery found we are going to rescue B.E.F from Belgium. Sailed late evening, passed burning Dunkirk very close and was machine gunned by C.M.B.

Tuesday 28th May 1940 Anchored off La Panne beach just after midnight. I spent six hours in boat to beach and back. Mostly transport on this trip and we took about 400 and landed them at Ramsgate. No sleep and only one meal, off again tonight.

Wednesday 29th May 1940 Went alongside the Mole and embarked another 400, mostly R.E. Poor devils done in. Dunkirk a very terrifying spectacle but easier to get the men aboard. Attacked several times by Jerry but scared him off. These pages too small to relate everything.

Thursday 30th May 1940 Landed our troops at Margate and back again for more. All over chaps exhausted and dropping down for half an hour sleep when they can. Took off infantry this time. Beach thick with them and Jerry bombed and shelled them all the time.

Friday 31st May 1940 A spell at last and I think we all just fell over in any old corner. Third Engineer finished, took him ashore. Heard Gracie Fields bombed and sunk and many killed.

Saturday 1st June 1940 Went over again to 1½ miles east of Dunkirk. Getting very warm now shrapnel fell all around us continuously. I think nearly all the BEF are away now. Many badly wounded this trip. One poor chap died in our own mess. Saw Massey Shaw.*

Sunday 2nd June 1940 Sailed again, this to be the last. Went into Dunkirk and embarked French troops. Just like being in the front line, shelled from every direction was very relieved to get away. Lots of wrecks about now.

Monday 3rd June 1940 Landed our troops at Ramsgate and went to Dover. Seems we are to make another trip yet. Went to Dunkirk and got another load of French soldiers. Not so bad tonight only long range guns. Nearly sunk by two transports.

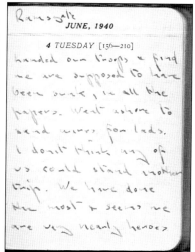

Tuesday 4th June 1940 Landed our troops and found we are supposed to have been sunk, in all the papers. Went ashore to send wires for lads. I don't think any of us could stand another trip. We have done the most...

and it seems we are very nearly heroes.

Wednesday 5th June 1940
En-route for Portsmouth and we are to get three days leave soon. Wonder if we shall go back to Dover, could do with a change. Had a lovely sleep and a bath today.

Thursday 6th June 1940
Arrived here after a rotten night at sea with aircraft scares galore. Hanging about outside for hours because of many mines. Went on leave.

* Thames fire boat.

Post Office Telegram

GREETINGS

119   GTG 11.14   RAMSGATE 17

SKINNER 89 COLES GREEN ROAD CRICKLEWOOD

NW 2 =

AM OK LOVE TO YOU BOTH PLEASE PHONE MUM

= JACK +

WELL DONE MEDWAY QUEEN

As a result of their endeavours throughout the evacuation, a number of *Medway Queen*'s crew received awards. The awards are listed in the London Gazette and it is thought the medals were presented by H.M. King George VI himself at Buckingham Palace.

The DSC was awarded to:

Lieutenant A.T. Cook RNR (Commanding Officer)
Sub-Lieutenant J. D. Graves RNR (First Lieutenant)

The DSM was awarded to:

Petty Officer A. E. Crossley RFR
Petty Officer H. J. McAllister RFR
Seaman K. R. Olley RNR

Mentioned in Despatches:

Second Engineer T. Irvine
Fireman J. D. Connell

In Admiral Ramsay's own words:
"WELL DONE MEDWAY QUEEN"

THE DUNKERQUE MEDAL

The Dunkerque Medal was created in 1960 by the town of Dunkerque to commemorate the actions of May and June 1940. It was initially awarded to French personnel but in 1970 it was also awarded to any allied member involved in operation Dynamo between 29th May and 3rd June including the civilian little ship volunteers and those soldiers evacuated.

Opposite page: HMS Medway Queen, Painted by Lionel Cook MBE, Alfred Cook's son.

Left: The medal awarded to Harold Slade - courtesy of Andrew and Tim Claringbull

MEDWAY QUEEN TODAY

After Dunkirk and subsequent repairs in Portsmouth Dockyard HMS *Medway Queen* rejoined the 10th Flotilla at Dover. After a few weeks they were relocated to the East Coast and re-organised. *Medway Queen* served in the 7th Flotilla until late in 1943 when she briefly became an accommodation ship. She was re-commissioned in April 1944 and joined the training establishment at Granton near Edinburgh. She served in this role until after the end of the war and was eventually rebuilt in Southampton and returned to civilian service in 1947. This ceased at the end of the 1963 season and after a couple of years of uncertainty she opened as a club house and restaurant at a marina on the Isle of Wight. This lasted until 1974 when she fell out of use. The ship was eventually purchased, refloated and taken back to the Medway for preservation in 1984. The Medway Queen Preservation Society was formed in 1985 and in 1987 they became the owners of the ship. In due course funding was obtained from the Heritage Lottery Fund and the hull was completely rebuilt in the Albion Dockyard, Bristol. She returned to Gillingham on the Medway in November 2013.

*Opposite: **Medway Queen** at Gillingham Pier - courtesy of Martin Goodhew.*

*Above: **Medway Queen** in Ramsgate harbour for the 75th anniversary of Dunkirk in 2015 - courtesy of Richard Halton.*

You can visit PS *Medway Queen* at Gillingham Pier, where She is open to the public on most Saturdays. Details are on the society's website.

www.medwayqueen.co.uk

On this same website you can find more information on the ship's history and details of the further reading available (below) relevant to the ship's fascinating history and the complexities of her rebuild in Bristol.

The New Medway Steam Packet Company (Medway Queen Preservation Society) is an entirely voluntary organisation and registered charity based in Gillingham, Kent. We are working to restore *Medway Queen* to operational condition in the long term, but as an intermediate step getting the ship to a state where she can be hired out for functions, events, meetings etc. It would be fantastic to have her steaming again in the future but that will take more volunteer effort and far more funds than are currently available. The project needs sponsors and more volunteers in both technical and non-technical roles. We need administrators and tour guides as much as we need fitters and carpenters. Contact the MQPS at Gillingham Pier, Pier Approach Road, Gillingham, Kent. ME7 1RX.

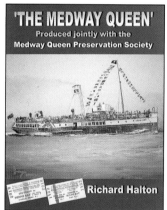

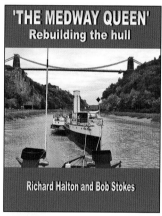

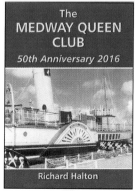